Quick After-Work

Curries

PAT CHAPMAN

FISHER
er
BOOKS™

Publishers:	Bill Fisher
	Howard Fisher
	Helen V. Fisher
North American Editors:	Helen V. Fisher
	Sarah Smith
Cover Design:	FifthStreet*design*
Book Design:	Josh Young
Illustrations:	Paul Saunders
Book Production:	Deanie Wood
Photography:	Steve Baxter
Nutrient Analysis:	Miriam Fisher

Library of Congress
Cataloging-in-Publication Data

Chapman, Pat, 1940-
    Quick after-work curries /
Pat Chapman.
        p. cm.
    Includes index.
    ISBN 1-55561-108-7 (pb)
    1. Cookery, Indic.   2. Quick and
easy cookery.   I. Title.
    TX724.5.I4C376   1996
    641.5954—dc20
                                96-23135
                                CIP

First published in Great Britain in
1995 by Piatkus Books, London
© 1995 Pat Chapman
The moral right of the author has
been asserted.

North American Edition
Published by Fisher Books
4239 W. Ina Road, Suite #101
Tucson, AZ 85741
(520) 744-6110

© 1996 Pat Chapman
Printed in USA
Printing 10 9 8 7 6 5 4 3 2

Contents

INTRODUCTION

People tell me they would love to get into curry making. The reason they don't is that they think it is too time-consuming, and after a busy day's work they haven't the inclination to bother.

Time is precious to everyone, yet curries need not take hours to make. And that's what this book is all about. The recipes will not have you slaving over a hot stove for half the day. They will give you superb-quality, delicious-tasting, spicy curry dishes with minimal time and effort. Any of them can be cooked in less than 30 minutes. Most take much less time.

The most time-consuming part of these recipes is assembling the ingredients and doing the preliminary slicing, dicing and chopping. If you do as much of this as possible the night or morning before, you can cook an entire meal consisting of several dishes in half an hour.

These are all recipes I have been making for as long as I can remember. And even though cooking and recipe-testing is my profession, when it comes to the after-work meal I do not wish to linger in the kitchen any more than any other busy person.

Some dishes are served cold and require no cooking. Most of the others are cooked on the stove. I avoided using the oven and deep fryer because they take so long to heat up. A few recipes use the broiler. All the recipes can be prepared without a microwave, but where there is an advantage to be gained by using one, I mention this.

In a number of recipes I have used prepared products—canned items or ready-made salads, for example, and anything that adds flavor but saves time. Dried onion flakes and bottled minced garlic are prime examples. A list of these useful "short-cut" ingredients and the spices you will need for your pantry is in chapter 1.

As for the recipes themselves, you will find many favorite names but you may be surprised at the different, rapid cooking methods. There is nothing "traditional" here—Indian home-cooking takes hours. Though time is saved, it is not at the expense of taste. In addition to your favorite curries you will find recipes using ingredients not normally associated with curry. They are well-tried and tested.

I have given both U.S. and metric measurements, but it is important to follow either one or the other. *Don't* mix U.S. and metric.

The portion size throughout is for two. Halve the ingredient quantities for one person, use one-and-a-half times the amounts for three, double them for four and so on. It will work every time. But enough of these practicalities. Without further ado, let's get on with the cooking!

PAT CHAPMAN

NUTRIENT ANALYSIS

Nutrient analysis was calculated using The Food Processor® for Windows software program, version 6.0, copyright 1987-1995 by ESHA Research.

Analysis does not include optional ingredients or variations. Where an ingredient amount is a range, the higher number is used. 2% milk was assumed in all recipes using milk.

The following abbreviations are used:
  Cal = Calories
  Prot = Protein
  Carb = Carbohydrates
  Fib = Fiber
  Tot. Fat = Total Fat
  Sat. Fat = Saturated Fat
  Chol = Cholesterol

Chapter One

ESSENTIALS

This chapter is about the all-important spices—and a few other ingredients—without which you cannot make curry. It includes recipes for the four spice mixtures used in the book—two curry powders (known in India as *masalas*); garam masala, which means "hot mixture of spices"; and Bengali five-spice mixture, a combination of seeds used in certain stir-fries.

You can buy ready-made versions of these mixtures, but you can easily make all four of them in a half hour or so. The fresh tastes they give the recipes are far superior to those of factory-made equivalents. I guarantee that once you have made your own spice mixtures you will continue to do so.

SPICES

Although the premise of this book is speed, I have not compromised on the variety of spices you will need to achieve the different tastes in these recipes. Spices are, after all, what curry is all about. The full list starts on page 8. Don't feel that you must buy all of them before you can make curries. Some are used in just one or two recipes. Start with those needed for Garam Masala, page 5, and Homemade Curry Powder, page 6. With just a few other ingredients you will be ready to try many different dishes.

Note: In the store, "chili powder" may mean either pure ground chile peppers or a blend of chiles and other ingredients. Indian cooking uses the pure ground chiles or cayenne pepper. Read the ingredient list on the label to make sure that is what you are buying.

There are two important rules in caring for spices:

First: Buy in small quantities. Spices deteriorate once their containers are opened and eventually lose all their flavor. Use ground spices within 6 to 12 months of opening; use whole ones within 12 to 18 months. Beyond those dates, throw them out and buy fresh.

Second: Store spices in airtight containers in a cool, dry, dark place. Keep them away from direct sunlight because this fades their colors and, more importantly, diminishes their flavors.

ROASTING SPICES—Roasting releases those delicious aromatic fragrances, the essential oils. To roast spices: Preheat a dry skillet or wok (no oil or water) over medium heat. Dry stir-fry whole spices for 30 to 60 seconds to release the aromas. Do not let the spices burn. If this happens, discard them and start again. Cool the spices. You can store them, but it is better to roast them just before using.

GRINDING SPICES—Roast the spices and let them cool. Then grind them with a mortar and pestle, if you enjoy hard work, or in a pepper mill, coffee grinder or blender.

FRESH HERBS

Relatively few fresh herbs are used in Indian cooking. Fresh cilantro leaves are the most popular. Every Indian garden has this member of the parsley family growing in it. It has a distinctive flavor; its ground seeds (coriander) produce a milder flavor.

Fresh mint, basil and curry leaves are also used in some recipes. A convenient way for after-work cooks to have these herbs available is to grow them in pots.

INGREDIENTS

Indian recipes include a variety of seasonings, which combine to give each dish its unique flavor. Omitting a hard-to-find ingredient may change the flavor slightly, but the result should still be very tasty. Prepared pickles, for example, are a standard staple in every Indian kitchen, but may be difficult to find here. Feel free to substitute a chutney.

The pantry list beginning on page 8 includes bottled substitutions for fresh ingredients, such as minced garlic and canned vegetables. These provide a good way to save preparation time and there is little difference in the outcome of the dish.

Most of the ingredients used in this book can be found in supermarkets and specialty stores. The others may be purchased by mail. Names and addresses of several mail-order suppliers are given on page 10.

See page 4 for recipes for some commonly used ingredients that are easy to make.

CLARIFIED BUTTER

Ghee, or clarified butter, may be purchased in specialty stores, but it is not difficult to make your own.

1. Place butter in medium nonstick pan. Melt over very low heat.

2. Raise heat slightly. Cook about 1 hour. Do not stir; keep heat low so it doesn't smoke or burn. Skim off the floating sediment with a slotted spoon.

3. Turn off heat and allow butter to cool a little. Strain it through cheesecloth or a paper coffee filter. Store in an airtight container. It will solidify, but remain soft. Clarified butter keeps for several months without refrigeration.

CREAMED COCONUT

Creamed coconut is a combination of freshly grated coconut meat and coconut oil and comes in a block. To use, melt desired amount in a little boiling water. Do not fry it without water; it will burn.

If creamed coconut is not available, substitute as follows: For 1 ounce creamed coconut, use 3 tablespoons coconut milk and 1 tablespoon grated coconut.

COCONUT MILK

Coconut milk *is not* the liquid inside a fresh coconut. It can be purchased in cans or in powdered form.

Or you can make your own: In a blender combine 1 cup shredded fresh or dried coconut and 1 cup hot water and blend 20 to 30 seconds. Let it steep for 30 minutes, then strain through a double layer of cheesecloth into a bowl. Squeeze the cheesecoth to remove as much milk as possible.

Coconut milk will keep up to 3 days in the refrigerator, longer in the freezer. One coconut will yield 2 to 4 cups milk.

GARAM MASALA

Garam means "hot" and *masala* means "mixture of spices." The heat comes from the black pepper. Garam masala is often used toward the end of the cooking. If added too early it may lose its aromatic qualities. It can also be sprinkled over a finished dish as a garnish.

There are as many different combinations as there are cooks. This is an aromatic version with easy-to-grind spices. Next time you may wish to add other spices or vary the quantities.

This recipe will season about 10 dishes for two people.

5 tablespoons (30g) coriander seeds
2 tablespoons (20g) cumin seeds
2 tablespoons (10g) fennel seeds
Cinnamon stick (2-inch / 5cm)

4-5 cardamom pods (10g)
2 teaspoons (10g) black peppercorns
2 teaspoons (10g) whole cloves

1. Combine spices in preheated wok or frying pan.
2. Dry stir-fry on medium heat for a minute or so, until a gorgeous aroma is given off.
3. Allow spices to cool, then grind them as finely as you can.
4. Store in an airtight container in a cool, dark place.

Makes about 7 tablespoons (100g).

HOMEMADE CURRY POWDER

Curry powder can be found in every supermarket the world over. Most cooks have it in their kitchen although some, it seems, rarely use it. You probably already have a favorite brand and if it is still fresh it will work in any of the recipes that call for curry powder.

I recommend that you make your own, in small quantities and often. Here's a 10-spice, easy-to-make mixture, enough for 10 double portions.

Whole Spices
2 teaspoons (10g) fennel seeds
Cinnamon stick (2-inch / 5cm)

2 teaspoons (10g) cloves
4-5 bay leaves (3g)

Ground Spices
5 tablespoons (80g) ground
  coriander
2 tablespoons (35g) ground cumin
2 tablespoons (30g) Garam
  Masala, page 5

1 tablespoon (15g) paprika
2 teaspoons (10g) turmeric
1-1/2 teaspoons (7g) chili powder

1. Combine whole spices in preheated wok or frying pan.
2. Dry stir-fry on medium heat for a minute or so, until a gorgeous aroma is given off.
3. Allow spices to cool, then grind them finely.
4. Mix in the ground spices.
5. Store in an airtight container in a cool, dark place.

Makes about 3/4 cup (200g).

TANDOORI CURRY POWDER

As with all homemade curry powders, this will improve during storage. Keep it in the dark in an airtight container and it will be good for up to 12 months. The bright reds and oranges that we associate with restaurant tandooris and tikkas are obtained through the use of artificial food colorings and are not authentic.

2 tablespoons (30g) tomato soup powder
2 tablespoons (30g) ground coriander
5 teaspoons (25g) ground cumin
5 teaspoons (25g) garlic powder

5 teaspoons (25g) paprika
4 teaspoons (20g) mango powder (optional)
6 teaspoons (20g) dried mint
3 teaspoons (15g) chili powder
2 teaspoons (10g) salt

1. Combine all ingredients and mix well.
2. Store in an airtight container in a cool, dark place.

Makes about 3/4 cup (200g).

BENGALI FIVE-SPICE MIXTURE

This mixture of whole spices is one of Bengal's most popular. Its secret is that each of the five spices adds a particular characteristic: fennel (aromatic), fenugreek (bitter), cumin (savory), nigella or black seed (sweet), mustard (pungent). Together they are musical.

fennel seeds
fenugreek seeds
cumin seeds

nigella (black seeds)
mustard seeds

1. Mix equal quantities together (1 teaspoon of each is plenty).
2. Store in an airtight container in a cool, dark place.

THE PANTRY

The following list includes all the nonperishable items used in the recipes in this book. Some items are used in only one recipe; others crop up again and again. Do not be confused by variations in the spelling of Indian words. Many of them were translated phonetically and there is no "correct" spelling in English.

Whole Spices

Bay leaves (Tej patia)
Cardamom (Elaichi)
Celery seeds (Ajowan)
Cinnamon stick (Dalchini)
Clove (Lavang)
Coriander seeds (Dhania)
Cumin seeds (Jeera)
Curry leaves (Neempatta or
    Kari phulia)
Fennel seeds (Soonf)

Fenugreek leaves
    (Tej methi kasoori)
Fenugreek seeds (Methi dhana)
Mustard seeds (Rai)
Nigella or black seeds (Kalonji)
Peppercorns (Kala mirch)
Poppy seeds, white (Cuscus)
Saffron stamens (Zafran)
Sesame seeds (Til)
Star anise (Badain or Kakraphol)

Ground Spices

Asafetida (Hing)
Chili powder (Lal mirch)
Chili powder, extra-hot or
    cayenne
Cinnamon, ground (Dalchini)
Clove, ground (Lavang)
Coriander, ground (Dhania)

Cumin, ground (Jeera)
Garlic powder (Lasan)
Mango powder (Amchoor)
Paprika (Paprika)
Saffron powder (Zafran)
Turmeric (Haldi)

Fresh Herbs

Basil
Chives
Cilantro

Curry plant
Mint

Oils

Clarified butter, or ghee
Hazelnut oil, olive oil
   and/or pistachio oil

Sesame oil
Soy oil and/or sunflower oil
Vegetable oil

General

Almonds
   ground
   sliced
Breadcrumbs
Cashews
Coconut
   creamed
   dried
Coconut milk
   canned
   unsweetened powder

Lentils, red split
Rice, basmati
Sugar
   dark brown or raw
   white
Tomato
   ketchup
   purée
   soup mix powder
Vinegar (any type)

Bottled Items

Basil, minced
Beets, pickled
Brinjal (eggplant) pickle (Indian)
Chili pickle (Indian)
Cilantro, dried
Crushed red pepper
Garlic, minced
Green peppercorns in brine
Hoisin sauce
Horseradish sauce
Lemon grass stalks
Lemon or lime juice
Lime pickle (Indian)
Mango chutney
Mango pickle (Indian)
Mint, dried

Mint jelly
Mustard
   Dijon-style
   dry
   prepared
Onion flakes
   dried
   toasted
Peanut butter
Pesto
Prawn balichow
Soy sauce
   dark
   light
Worcestershire sauce

Canned Items

Chickpeas (garbanzos)
Crabmeat
Hummus
Kidney beans, red
Lychees
Mushroom soup, cream of
Onion soup, French
Pineapple

Potatoes
Ratatouille
Shrimp
Tomato soup, cream of
Tomatoes, plum
Vegetables, mixed
Vichyssoise (or cream of leek and
    potato soup)

MAIL-ORDER SUPPLIERS OF INDIAN SPICES

Bazaar of India
1810 University Avenue
Berkeley, CA 94703
TEL: 800-261-7662
    510-548-4110

Nancy's Specialty Market
P.O. Box 530
Newmarket, NH 03857
TEL: 800-462-6291

Cinnabar Specialty Foods, Inc.
1134 West Haining Street
Prescott, AZ 86301
TEL: 800-824-4563
    520-778-3687
FAX: 520-778-4289

Penzey's, Ltd
P.O. Box 1448
Waukesha, WI 53187
TEL: 414-574-0277
FAX: 414-574-0278

Dean and DeLuca
Mail Order Department
560 Broadway
New York, NY 10012
TEL: 800-221-7714
($3.00 charge for catalog)

Spices, etc.
P.O. Box 5266
Charlottesville, VA 22905
TEL: 800-827-6373
FAX: 800-827-0145

Opposite: Chile-and-Pepper Steak (page 54) served with Bombay Potatoes
(page 82) and Kashmiri Salad (page 16)

Chapter Two

SALADS, SOUPS AND SNACKS

The recipes in this chapter are really quick. For speed in preparation, begin with ready-prepared salad greens, packaged mixed bean sprouts or leftovers from your refrigerator. Seven recipes require no cooking; the others just a little. Hot or cold, they can be enjoyed as snacks or as a prelude to a main dish.

Opposite: Ground Turkey Curry (page 65) served with Kitchri (page 103) and Spiced Shredded Vegetable Salad (page 15)

BEAN SPROUT MASALA MEDLEY

Many supermarkets sell attractive packages of mixed bean sprouts. Generally these consist of green and yellow lentils, chickpeas and soybeans. With their mix of shapes and colors as well as their different flavors, these sprouts make an attractive and highly nutritious salad. Add spices, and they are heavenly.

1/2 cup (145g) mixed bean
   sprouts
2 tablespoons cottage cheese
2 tablespoons plain yogurt
2 teaspoons chopped bell pepper
1/2 teaspoon minced green chile
   pepper

2 teaspoons Garam Masala,
   page 5
1/2 teaspoon Homemade Curry
   Powder, page 6
Salt to taste

1. Mix all ingredients together in a bowl.
2. Chill up to 24 hours if you have time, or serve at once.

Makes 2 servings.

Each serving contains:

Cal	Prot	Carb	Fib	Tot. Fat	Sat. Fat	Chol	Sodium
50	4g	6g	2g	2g	1g	4mg	200mg

SPICY SPAGHETTI OR NOODLES

What do you do with leftover spaghetti or noodles? I make them into an appetizing cold snack. This recipe is so tasty that it is worth cooking extra spaghetti or noodles for next-day use.

*2 tablespoons hazelnut oil or
   other nut oil*
1 tablespoon olive oil
*6 oz. (170g) cooked and cooled
   spaghetti or egg noodles*
*1 teaspoon Homemade Curry
   Powder, page 6*

2 teaspoons Garam Masala, page 5
1-3 green chile peppers, chopped
1 tablespoon chopped cilantro
1 tablespoon chopped mint
Salt to taste
Mixed salad greens
2 lemon slices

1. Pour oils over cold spaghetti or noodles and mix well.
2. Add remaining ingredients except greens and lemon slices. Toss well.
3. Serve on a bed of salad greens with a slice of lemon.

Makes 2 servings.

Variation
   Add shredded cooked beef, chopped chicken or small shrimp.

Each serving contains:

Cal	Prot	Carb	Fib	Tot. Fat	Sat. Fat	Chol	Sodium
361	7g	37g	6g	22g	2g	0mg	159mg

SPICY COTTAGE CHEESE

India's cheese, called *paneer,* is similar to cottage cheese, though more salty. Here is a simple and tasty cold snack. Serve with salads and cold dishes from this chapter, or use as a sandwich spread.

5 oz. (145g) cottage cheese
   (2/3 cup)
2 teaspoons Garam Masala,
   page 5
	1 green chile pepper, chopped
	   (optional)

1. Combine all ingredients in a bowl.
2. Chill up to 24 hours if you have time, or serve at once.

Makes 2 servings.

Each serving contains:

Cal	Prot	Carb	Fib	Tot. Fat	Sat. Fat	Chol	Sodium
86	9g	5g	1g	4g	2g	10mg	287mg

SPICED SHREDDED VEGETABLE SALAD

Supermarkets offer mouthwatering, ready-prepared salads to save you time and waste. This recipe elevates humble shredded carrot and cabbage (coleslaw minus the salad dressing), salad greens and green onions to something special. You could choose other salad options if you wish.

3/4 cup (60g) mixed salad greens, shredded
3-4 green onions (leaves and bulbs), shredded
2/3 cup (145g) shredded carrot-and-cabbage mixture
1 red chile pepper, chopped (optional)

2 tablespoons olive oil
1 tablespoon sunflower oil
2 tablespoons lemon or lime juice
2 teaspoons Garam Masala, page 5
1 teaspoon Homemade Curry Powder, page 6
Salt to taste

1. Combine all ingredients in a bowl.
2. Chill up to 2 hours if you have time, or serve at once.

Makes 2 servings.

Each serving contains:

Cal	Prot	Carb	Fib	Tot. Fat	Sat. Fat	Chol	Sodium
222	2g	9g	4g	22g	3g	0mg	156mg

KASHMIRI SALAD

A quick and delicious combination of salad vegetables with yogurt, spices and a hint of mayonnaise.

4-6 green onions (leaves and bulbs), chopped
4-6 radicchio leaves, shredded
1 tablespoon shredded bell pepper
1-2 tomatoes, chopped
1-2 green chile peppers, chopped

1 tablespoon chopped pickled beet
1 tablespoon Garam Masala, page 5
3-4 tablespoons plain yogurt
2-3 teaspoons mayonnaise
Salt to taste

1. Combine all ingredients in a nonmetallic bowl.
2. Chill up to 6 hours if you have time, or serve at once.

Makes 2 servings.

Each serving contains:

Cal	Prot	Carb	Fib	Tot. Fat	Sat. Fat	Chol	Sodium
157	5g	21g	5g	8g	2g	8mg	237mg

CURRIED RICE SALAD

Curried rice salad is particularly delicious. I include tasty enhancements such as cumin seeds, garam masala and chile peppers.

*1 cup (225g) cooked and cooled
   basmati rice
1/2 teaspoon cumin seeds
1 tablespoon nut oil
2-3 green onions (bulbs and
   leaves), chopped
1-2 red chile peppers, chopped
6 tablespoons plain yogurt*

*1 tablespoon mayonnaise
1 tablespoon Homemade Curry
   Powder, page 6, or Tandoori
   Curry Powder, page 7
1 teaspoon Garam Masala, page 5
Salt to taste
Garnishes—chopped pistachios,
   cilantro*

1. Combine salad ingredients in a bowl. Top with garnishes.
2. Chill if you have time, or serve at once.

Makes 2 servings.

Each serving contains:

Cal	Prot	Carb	Fib	Tot. Fat	Sat. Fat	Chol	Sodium
321	7g	34g	4g	19g	3g	10mg	207mg

CURRIED PÂTÉ

This really works well and is so easy! Serve on hot buttered toast (or with hot naan bread) and with one of the salads in this chapter.

4 oz. (115g) pâté (any type) *1/2 teaspoon chili powder*
2 teaspoons Garam Masala, page 5 *(optional)*

1. Place pâté in a bowl, discarding any aspic or skin.
2. Mix in remaining ingredients.

Makes 2 servings.

Each serving contains:

Cal	Prot	Carb	Fib	Tot. Fat	Sat. Fat	Chol	Sodium
128	8g	6g	2g	8g	2g	222mg	223mg

CHILLED PEPPER WATER

If you like tomato juice with a dash of Worcestershire sauce, as I do, you will enjoy this as a refreshing alternative on a hot summer evening—or at any time.

2 teaspoons soy or sunflower oil
1 teaspoon ground coriander
1/2 teaspoon ground cumin
1/4 teaspoon mango powder
  (optional)
1/2 to 1 teaspoon chili powder

1-1/2 cups (375ml) cold vegetable
  stock or water
1/2 cup (125ml) tomato juice
1/2 teaspoon Worcestershire sauce
1 tablespoon chopped fresh mint
Salt to taste

1. Heat oil in a skillet. Add spices and stir-fry about 30 seconds. Remove pan from heat.
2. Add vegetable stock or water, tomato juice, Worcestershire sauce, mint and salt.
3. Put crushed ice into 2 glasses and pour pepper water into each one, stirring well.

Makes 2 servings.

Each serving contains:

Cal	Prot	Carb	Fib	Tot. Fat	Sat. Fat	Chol	Sodium
82	2g	9g	2g	5g	1g	0mg	391mg

PAPPADUMS

Pappadums are wafer-thin East Indian flatbreads made with lentil flour. They may be flavored with red or black pepper, garlic or other seasonings, or unseasoned, as preferred in southern India. They can be deep-fried, causing them to puff up almost double, or grilled over an open flame to give a smoky flavor.

Pappadums are the most satisfying of all preludes to an Indian meal. I like to munch my way through them accompanied by at least one chutney, chapter 11, while I cook my main curry meal. Instead of deep-frying them, try one of these quick ways to cook pappadums. If pappadums are not available in your supermarket, substitute Mexican tortillas.

The Broiler
Preheat broiler and place rack in the middle of the oven. Broil 1 or 2 pappadums at a time for about 10 seconds. Ensure that the edges are cooked. Because they are oil-free they can be served at once or stored until needed.

The Microwave
Pappadums can also be microwaved. Cook 2 pappadums on full power about 30 seconds. Inspect and heat longer if necessary. Serve at once or store until needed.
Allow 2 to 3 per person.

SHRIMP PATIA

Patia is a Parsee curry, traditionally made with a thick, dark-brown, sweet-and-sour sauce. This stir-fried version is slightly sweet, yet contrastingly hot and tangy. Serve with rolls, lemon wedges and a side salad.

2 tablespoons clarified butter or
   vegetable oil
1/2 teaspoon cumin seeds
1/2 teaspoon fennel seeds
2 teaspoons minced garlic
1 tablespoon Homemade Curry
   Powder, page 6
1 tablespoon Tandoori Curry
   Powder, page 7
6 tablespoons dried onion flakes

1/2 cup (125ml) water
1 can (8-10 oz. / 225-280g)
   shrimp
1 tablespoon ketchup
1 tablespoon tomato purée
1 tablespoon coconut-milk powder
1 tablespoon brown sugar
2 teaspoons prawn balichow
1/2 teaspoon dried cilantro
Salt to taste

1. Heat butter or oil in a skillet and stir-fry seeds 10 seconds. Add garlic and continue stir-frying 1 minute. Add curry powders and cook 1 minute longer.
2. Add onion flakes, stirring briskly until they absorb the oil and start sizzling. Add water and bring to a simmer.
3. Add remaining ingredients except salt. Simmer 5 minutes, until sauce has thickened. Add salt.

Makes 2 servings.

Each serving contains:

Cal	Prot	Carb	Fib	Tot. Fat	Sat. Fat	Chol	Sodium
635	38g	32g	6g	43g	29g	278mg	739mg

SPICY POTATO FRITTERS

This is a wonderful way to use up cooked potatoes. Mashed, spiced and fried, they are transformed into delicious fritters. Serve with pickles and a salad.

4-6 large potatoes, cooked
1-2 teaspoons Homemade Curry
  Powder, page 6
1 teaspoon minced garlic
1 teaspoon cumin seeds
1-3 green chile peppers, minced

1 tablespoon chopped cilantro
1/2 teaspoon salt
Milk or water
1 egg
4-6 tablespoons breadcrumbs
4 tablespoons vegetable oil

1. Mash potatoes with curry powder, garlic, cumin seeds, chile peppers, cilantro and salt.
2. Divide into 4 balls, moistening with a little milk or water if necessary. Shape each ball into a flat round or sausage shape.
3. In a small bowl, whisk egg with a fork. Spread breadcrumbs on a cutting board.
4. Coat potato fritters with egg, then cover with breadcrumbs.
5. Heat oil in a skillet and fry fritters about 5 minutes, turning them frequently.

Makes 4 fritters.

Variation

Add 2 or 3 tablespoons of peas and/or chopped ham in step 1.

Each fritter contains:

Cal	Prot	Carb	Fib	Tot. Fat	Sat. Fat	Chol	Sodium
376	7g	52g	4g	16g	3g	54mg	582mg

SPICY TOMATO SOUP

This is so simple, you could call it cheating! Simply open the can, heat the soup and add the spices. I serve it often.

1 can (14-oz. / 400ml) cream of tomato soup
1 can (14-oz. / 400ml) water or milk
1 tablespoon vinegar
1 teaspoon Worcestershire sauce
1/4 teaspoon ground cumin

1/4 teaspoon ground coriander
1/2 teaspoon Garam Masala, page 5
1/2 teaspoon chili powder (optional)
Salt to taste
Cream or half-and-half
Chopped chives, dill or cilantro

1. Heat soup and water or milk in a saucepan.
2. Add vinegar, Worcestershire sauce, spices and salt and bring to a simmer.
3. Garnish with swirls of cream or half-and-half and fresh herbs.

Makes 2 servings.

Each serving contains:

Cal	Prot	Carb	Fib	Tot. Fat	Sat. Fat	Chol	Sodium
241	10g	27g	0g	11g	7g	33mg	419mg

SPICY TOMATO JUICE

This lighter version of the previous recipe uses tomato juice. It can be served hot or cold.

1 tablespoon vinegar
1 teaspoon Worcestershire sauce
1/4 teaspoon ground cumin
1/4 teaspoon ground coriander
1/2 teaspoon Garam Masala, page 5

1/2 teaspoon chili powder
 (optional)
1 can (14-oz. / 400ml) tomato
 juice
Salt to taste

1. Combine all ingredients in saucepan and heat, stirring well.

2. Serve hot, or add ice, preferably crushed, and serve chilled.

Makes 2 servings.

Each serving contains:

Cal	Prot	Carb	Fib	Tot. Fat	Sat. Fat	Chol	Sodium
43	2g	11g	1g	0g	0g	0mg	933mg

VEGETABLE RASAM SOUP

This is an imaginative and easy way to use up leftover vegetables.

2 tablespoons clarified butter or sesame oil
1/2 teaspoon cumin seeds
1/2 teaspoon mustard seeds
1/2 teaspoon sesame seeds
1 to 2 teaspoons minced garlic
2 teaspoons Homemade Curry Powder, page 6
1-1/2 cups (375ml) water

1/2 cup (85g) mixed cooked vegetables, chopped
2 tablespoons chopped cilantro
10-12 curry leaves, fresh or dried (optional)
1-2 red chile peppers, chopped (optional)
Salt to taste

1. Heat butter or oil in a saucepan. Stir-fry seeds 20 seconds. Add garlic and curry powder and stir-fry 1 minute.
2. Add water and bring to a simmer.
3. Add vegetables, cilantro, curry leaves and chiles, if using, and bring to a simmer. Add salt, strain if you wish, and serve hot.

Makes 2 servings.

Each serving contains:

Cal	Prot	Carb	Fib	Tot. Fat	Sat. Fat	Chol	Sodium
164	2g	9g	4g	15g	2g	0mg	160mg

Chapter Three

INSTANT TANDOORIS
AND TIKKAS

Tandoori is a style of cooking in which meat is marinated in a red yogurt sauce and then baked over charcoal in a clay oven called a *tandoor*. Tikka is similar, except that pieces of the marinated meat are placed on skewers. They may be baked in the tandoor or barbecued on a grill.

Here is a totally new approach to tandooris and tikkas, which normally are marinated for a day or two—and who thinks that far ahead in a busy workweek? These instant, nonmarinated versions are almost indistinguishable from the 60-hour ones!

MEAT TIKKA

Pieces of meat are traditionally marinated, then skewered and baked. This recipe dispenses with the marinade. Because the meat is cut into small pieces it can be stir-fried to achieve almost as good a result in a fraction of the time. Serve with a side salad and raita.

3 tablespoons vegetable oil
2 teaspoons minced garlic
2 tablespoons Tandoori Curry
   Powder, page 7
3 tablespoons water

2 tablespoons tomato purée
10-12 oz. (280-340g) cubed
   steak, cut into strips
1/4 teaspoon Garam Masala, page 5
1/4 teaspoon salt

1. Heat oil in wok or large skillet. Stir-fry garlic 20 seconds, then add curry powder, continuing to stir-fry 1 minute longer. Add water, mixing it in well, then add tomato purée.
2. Add meat, turning to coat with mixture. Stir-fry 3 to 5 minutes, until cooked as desired.
3. Sprinkle with garam masala and salt and serve.

Makes 2 servings.

Each serving contains:

Cal	Prot	Carb	Fib	Tot. Fat	Sat. Fat	Chol	Sodium
495	42g	10g	3g	32g	7g	115mg	845mg

TANDOORI LAMB CHOPS

Chops are coated and broiled, and immediately enjoyed with a side salad and a chutney. They are also good cooked on the grill.

4 lamb or pork chops,
  each 4 oz. (115g)
1/4 cup (60g) plain yogurt
1 tablespoon vegetable oil
1 tablespoon lemon juice
1 teaspoon minced garlic
1/2 teaspoon chili powder

1/2 teaspoon Garam Masala, page 5
1 tablespoon Tandoori Curry
  Powder, page 7
1 tablespoon tomato purée
1/4 teaspoon salt
1/4 cup (60ml) milk

1. Trim fat from chops and make small gashes around edge of chops.
2. Combine remaining ingredients in a nonmetallic bowl.
3. Dredge chops in mixture, turning until well coated.
4. Preheat broiler and line broiler pan with foil. Put rack over foil. Place chops on the rack and broil about 5 minutes.
5. Turn chops over and baste with remaining coating mixture. Broil another 3 minutes or until cooked as desired.

Makes 2 servings.

Each serving contains:

Cal	Prot	Carb	Fib	Tot. Fat	Sat. Fat	Chol	Sodium
691	49g	9g	2g	51g	19g	185mg	687mg

CHICKEN TIKKA

As with the recipe for Meat Tikka, page 28, this one for chicken omits the traditional marinating, skewering and baking and gives an almost-instant result. Serve with salads, bread and a chutney or two. Note the use of wine, if you happen to have some on hand.

10-12 oz. (280-340g) boned,
   skinned chicken breasts
2 tablespoons vegetable oil
2 teaspoons minced garlic
2 tablespoons Tandoori Curry
   Powder, page 7

2 tablespoons tomato purée
1/4 teaspoon salt
Red wine (optional)

1. Cut chicken into bite-size pieces.
2. Combine remaining ingredients in a large bowl, then add the chicken pieces, turning until well coated.
3. Heat wok or large skillet. Add chicken and sauce and stir-fry over medium heat 10 to 15 minutes, until chicken is cooked. Add a tablespoon or two of water or red wine as needed to prevent sticking.

Makes 2 servings.

Variation

Shrimp Tikka—Instead of chicken, use 3/4 pound (340g) shelled shrimp.

Each serving contains:

Cal	Prot	Carb	Fib	Tot. Fat	Sat. Fat	Chol	Sodium
355	37g	10g	3g	19g	3g	94mg	841mg

TANDOORI TROUT

Coat the fish with a yogurt-based tandoori-flavored coating and broil them—or move outside to the gas grill for a summer barbecue. Serve with salad, lemon wedges, bread or a rice dish and chutneys.

2 fresh trout, each 3/4 lb. (340g)
2/3 cup (145g) plain yogurt
2 tablespoons Tandoori Curry
    Powder, page 7

2 tablespoons tomato purée
1/4 teaspoon salt

1. Rinse trout and pat dry.
2. Combine remaining ingredients in a bowl; coat trout with most of mixture.
3. Preheat broiler and line broiler pan with foil. Place rack over foil and place coated trout on rack. Place pan in middle of oven and broil 10 to 12 minutes. Turn trout at least once and baste with remaining spice mixture.
4. To finish, place pan closer to heat until trout begin to blacken.

Makes 2 servings.

Each serving contains:

Cal	Prot	Carb	Fib	Tot. Fat	Sat. Fat	Chol	Sodium
389	52g	12g	2g	14g	4g	144mg	952mg

CHICKEN TIKKA MASALA CURRY

Chicken Tikka Masala is tangy rather than hot, savory but sweet, creamy and colorful. The gravy is made while you cook the stir-fry. Serve with a rice dish. Don't be put off by the long list of ingredients. Once assembled, the whole curry takes only 15 minutes to cook.

2 tablespoons vegetable oil
1 tablespoon Tandoori Curry
   Powder, page 7
2 tablespoons tomato purée
3 tablespoons plain yogurt
3/4 lb. (340g) boned, skinned
   chicken breasts, cubed
2 tablespoons clarified butter or
   vegetable oil
1/2 teaspoon cumin seeds
1/2 teaspoon mustard seeds
1 tablespoon Tandoori Curry
   Powder, page 7
2 teaspoons Homemade Curry
   Powder, page 6
2 teaspoons minced garlic
3 tablespoons dried onion flakes

1 teaspoon dried fenugreek leaves
1 teaspoon dried mint leaves
2-3 canned plum tomatoes,
   chopped
6-8 tablespoons canned cream of
   tomato soup
2 tablespoons chopped bell pepper
1-2 green chile peppers, chopped
1/4 cup (60ml) cream
1 oz. (30g) creamed coconut,
   chopped, page 4
1 teaspoon Garam Masala, page 5
1 teaspoon sugar
1 tablespoon chopped cilantro
Garnishes—cream, cilantro
   leaves, sliced almonds

Each serving contains:

Cal	Prot	Carb	Fib	Tot. Fat	Sat. Fat	Chol	Sodium
812	44g	38g	8g	58g	25g	191mg	666mg

1. Combine oil, curry powder, tomato purée and yogurt in a large bowl. Add chicken pieces, turning until well coated.
2. Heat wok or large skillet. Cook chicken over medium heat 8 to 10 minutes, stirring often.
3. In a separate pan, heat butter or vegetable oil and stir-fry seeds and curry powders 20 seconds. Add garlic and cook 30 seconds longer. Add onion flakes, fenugreek and mint and stir-fry briskly. Add tomatoes and tomato soup and bring to a simmer. Add peppers and simmer about 5 minutes. If mixture seems too dry, add a little water.
4. Add this mixture and remaining ingredients, except garnishes, to chicken. Stir-fry about 5 minutes.
5. Garnish with swirls of cream, cilantro and almonds.

Makes 2 servings.

BEEF TIKKA MASALA CURRY

Like the previous recipe, this one cooks in 15 minutes. Use a good cut of meat to achieve tenderness. Serve with a rice dish.

2 tablespoons vegetable oil
1 tablespoon Tandoori Curry
    Powder, page 7
2 tablespoons tomato purée
3 tablespoons plain yogurt
3/4 lb. (340g) boneless beef, cut
    in 1-inch (2.5cm) cubes
2 tablespoons clarified butter or
    vegetable oil
1/2 teaspoon cumin seeds
1/2 teaspoon mustard seeds
1 tablespoon Tandoori Curry
    Powder, page 7
2 teaspoons Homemade Curry
    Powder, page 6
2 teaspoons minced garlic
3 tablespoons dried onion flakes

1 teaspoon dried fenugreek leaves
1 teaspoon dried mint
2-3 canned plum tomatoes,
    chopped
6-8 tablespoons canned cream of
    tomato soup
2 tablespoons chopped bell pepper
1-2 green chile peppers, chopped
1/4 cup (60ml) cream
1 oz. (30g) creamed coconut,
    chopped, page 4
1 teaspoon Garam Masala, page 5
1 teaspoon sugar
1 tablespoon chopped cilantro
Garnishes—cream, cilantro
    leaves, sliced almonds

Each serving contains:

Cal	Prot	Carb	Fib	Tot. Fat	Sat. Fat	Chol	Sodium
891	49g	38g	8g	64g	28g	212mg	669mg

1. Combine oil, curry powder, tomato purée and yogurt in a large bowl. Add meat, turning until well coated.
2. Heat wok or large skillet. Stir-fry meat 6 to 8 minutes.
3. In a separate pan, heat butter or oil and stir-fry seeds and curry powders 20 seconds. Add garlic and stir-fry 30 seconds. Add onion flakes, fenugreek and mint and stir-fry briskly. Add tomatoes and tomato soup, bring to a simmer and add peppers. Simmer 5 minutes. If mixture becomes too dry, add a little water.
4. Add this mixture and remaining ingredients, except garnishes, to meat. Stir-fry 5 minutes.
5. Garnish with swirls of cream, cilantro leaves and almonds.

Makes 2 servings.

Variation

Shrimp Tikka Masala Curry—Instead of beef, use 3/4 pound (340g) shelled shrimp.

CHICKEN TIKKA OMELET

This combines chicken and eggs in a novel way. I suggest you make this omelet when you have leftover chicken tikka in the refrigerator. Serve with salad and fresh rolls, french fries or potato sticks.

4 large eggs
1 red chile pepper, chopped
1 tablespoon chopped cilantro
Ground black pepper, to taste
1/4 teaspoon salt

1/2 cup (115g) Chicken Tikka,
*   page 30, chopped*
1 tablespoon butter
Garnishes—snipped chives,
*   Garam Masala, page 5*

1. Whisk eggs in a bowl. Add chile pepper, cilantro, black pepper and salt, mixing well.
2. Heat chicken by stir-frying or microwaving it.
3. Heat butter in a skillet. When it has melted pour off the excess into another pan.
4. Give egg mixture a final whisk, then pour half of it into skillet. Roll egg mixture around the pan with a quick wrist action. Return to the heat. When it begins to set, add half the hot chicken.
5. Cook about 1 minute, then slide omelet out of pan, roll or fold it up and keep warm.
6. Make second omelet with remaining ingredients.
7. Garnish with chives and garam masala.

Makes 2 servings.

Each serving contains:

Cal	Prot	Carb	Fib	Tot. Fat	Sat. Fat	Chol	Sodium
265	18g	7g	2g	19g	7g	452mg	564mg

Chapter Four

INSTANT BALTIS

Baltis were originally slow-cooked dishes from the northernmost part of Pakistan. Now they have evolved into rapid stir-fries, so are most suitable for this book. Traditionally they are cooked and served in a two-handled pan—the balti pan or *karahi*—and eaten with naan bread. If you have such a pan it adds to the fun. Use a 10-inch (25cm) balti pan, serve out of it and accompany with warm pita or naan bread and chutneys.

Baltis are fun because you can combine anything with anything. They are good recipes for using leftover vegetables. The balti flavor comes from the combination of curry powder and garam marsala.

BALTI MEAT

Cooking time is minimized by using small pieces of meat. Serve with naan or pita bread and chutneys.

4 tablespoons clarified butter or vegetable oil
1/2 teaspoon cumin seeds
1/2 teaspoon fennel seeds
1/4 teaspoon cardamom seeds
2 teaspoons minced garlic
1 teaspoon minced fresh ginger
1 tablespoon Homemade Curry Powder, page 6
1 tablespoon Garam Masala, page 5
6 tablespoons dried onion flakes
1/3 cup (80ml) tomato juice

1/4 cup (60ml) red wine or water
12-14 oz. (340-400g) fillet steak, cubed (1 x 1/2 inch / 2.5x1.3cm)
1 tablespoon chopped bell pepper
1 green chile pepper, chopped (optional)
1 teaspoon dried fenugreek leaves
2 tablespoons plain yogurt
1 tablespoon chopped cilantro
Salt to taste
Garnish—cilantro leaves

Each serving contains:

Cal	Prot	Carb	Fib	Tot. Fat	Sat. Fat	Chol	Sodium
648	49g	21g	6g	40g	21g	202mg	404mg

1. Heat half the butter or oil in wok or large skillet. Stir-fry seeds 20 seconds. Add garlic and ginger and cook 30 seconds more. Add remaining butter or oil, curry powder and garam masala.
2. Add onion flakes and stir-fry briskly. Add tomato juice and red wine or water. Bring to a simmer and add meat, peppers and fenugreek leaves.
3. Stir-fry 5 minutes, then add yogurt and chopped cilantro.
4. Cook another 5 minutes, until meat is cooked, adding more water if necessary to prevent sticking.
5. Add salt, garnish with cilantro leaves and serve.

Makes 2 servings.

Variation

Balti Chicken—Omit beef and substitute cubed boned, skinned chicken or turkey.

BALTI FISH

Cod or haddock fillets are ideal choices for this recipe. They stir-fry well, which means they cook quickly and do not break up.

3 tablespoons soy or sunflower oil
1/2 teaspoon fennel seeds
1/2 teaspoon mustard seeds
1/4 teaspoon celery seeds
3 teaspoons minced garlic
2-1/2 teaspoons Homemade Curry
*   Powder, page 6*
1/2 teaspoon turmeric
1 tablespoon Garam Masala, page 5
6 tablespoons dried onion flakes
1/3 cup (80ml) milk

1 oz. (30g) creamed coconut,
*   chopped, page 4*
14 oz. (400g) cod or haddock fillets,
*   cut in 1-inch (2.5cm) pieces*
1 tablespoon chopped bell pepper
1 red chile pepper, chopped
2 tablespoons cream
1 tablespoon chopped cilantro
Salt to taste
Garnishes—cilantro leaves, dried
*   coconut*

1. Heat half the oil in wok or large skillet. Stir-fry seeds 20 seconds. Add garlic and stir-fry 30 seconds. Add remaining oil, curry powder, turmeric and garam masala.
2. Add onion flakes and stir-fry briskly. Add milk and creamed coconut. Bring to a simmer and add fish and peppers.
3. Stir-fry 5 minutes, then add cream and chopped cilantro.
4. Continue cooking 5 minutes, until fish is cooked, adding more water if necessary to prevent sticking.
5. Add salt, garnish with cilantro leaves and coconut, and serve.

Makes 2 servings.

Each serving contains:

Cal	Prot	Carb	Fib	Tot. Fat	Sat. Fat	Chol	Sodium
532	35g	21g	6g	37g	12g	96mg	269mg

BALTI SHRIMP

If you have any leftover cooked shrimp, chop them for this recipe.

3 tablespoons soy or sunflower oil
1/2 teaspoon fennel seeds
1/2 teaspoon mustard seeds
1/4 teaspoon celery seeds
3 teaspoons minced garlic
2-1/2 teaspoons Homemade Curry
   Powder, page 6
1/2 teaspoon turmeric
1 tablespoon Garam Masala, page 5
6 tablespoons dried onion flakes
1 oz. (30g) creamed coconut,
   chopped, page 4
1/3 cup (80ml) milk

14 oz. (400g) small cooked,
   peeled shrimp or 1 can
   (12-oz. / 340g) small shrimp
1 tablespoon chopped bell pepper
1-2 red chile peppers, chopped
1/2 teaspoon dried fenugreek
   leaves
2 tablespoons cream
1 tablespoon chopped cilantro
Salt to taste
Garnishes—cilantro leaves, dried
   coconut

1. Heat half the oil in wok or large skillet. Stir-fry seeds 20 seconds. Add garlic and continue to cook 30 seconds longer. Add remaining oil, curry powder, turmeric and garam masala.
2. Add onion flakes and stir-fry briskly. Add creamed coconut and milk. Bring to a simmer and add shrimp, peppers and fenugreek.
3. Cook 5 minutes, then add cream and chopped cilantro.
4. Cook and stir until shrimp are heated, adding more water if necessary to prevent sticking.
5. Add salt, garnish with cilantro leaves and coconut, and serve.

Makes 2 servings.

Each serving contains:

Cal	Prot	Carb	Fib	Tot. Fat	Sat. Fat	Chol	Sodium
545	36g	23g	7g	37g	12g	305mg	503mg

CORN-AND-MUSHROOM STIR-FRY

The balti flavor comes from the combination of curry powder and garam masala. Fresh mushrooms bring the dish alive.

1 can (8-oz. / 225g) corn kernels
2 tablespoons clarified butter or
   sesame oil
1/2 teaspoon cumin seeds
1/2 teaspoon fennel seeds
2 teaspoons minced garlic
1 teaspoon minced fresh ginger
1 tablespoon Homemade Curry
   Powder, page 6
1 tablespoon Garam Masala, page 5

2 tablespoons dried onion flakes
6 oz. (170g) fresh mushrooms,
   chopped or sliced (3/4 cup)
4-6 green onions (bulbs and
   leaves), chopped
2-3 canned tomatoes, chopped
2 tablespoons chopped bell pepper
2-3 green chile peppers, chopped
Salt to taste

1. Drain corn, reserving liquid. Add water to make 1/3 cup (80ml).
2. Heat butter or oil in wok or large skillet and stir-fry seeds 10 seconds. Add garlic and ginger and stir-fry 1 minute. Add curry powder and garam masala and cook 1 minute longer.
3. Add onion flakes, stirring briskly until they start sizzling. Add reserved corn liquid and remaining ingredients except salt. Simmer 2 to 3 minutes, then add salt to taste.

Makes 2 servings.

Each serving contains:

Cal	Prot	Carb	Fib	Tot. Fat	Sat. Fat	Chol	Sodium
304	8g	43g	9g	15g	8g	33mg	779mg

Opposite: Corn-and-Mushroom Stir-Fry (above) served with Madrasi Sambar (page 83) and White Coconut Raita (page 109)

VEGETABLE MEDLEY

Baltis are fun because you can combine anything with anything. They are good recipes for using leftover vegetables.

3 tablespoons vegetable oil
1 teaspoon cumin seeds
2 teaspoons minced garlic
1 tablespoon Homemade Curry
  Powder, page 6
6 tablespoons dried onion flakes
1/3 cup (80ml) tomato juice
1 stalk celery, sliced
1/3 cup (85g) sugar peas
1/3 cup (85g) carrots, sliced
3-4 canned or cooked new
  potatoes, quartered

3-4 cherry tomatoes, halved
1/3 cup (85g) peas
1 tablespoon chopped bell pepper
1-2 green chile peppers, chopped
1 teaspoon dried fenugreek leaves
2 tablespoons plain yogurt
1 teaspoon Garam Masala, page 5
2 teaspoons chopped cilantro
Salt to taste
Garnishes—cilantro leaves,
  shredded carrot

1. Heat oil in wok or skillet. Stir-fry cumin seeds 20 seconds, add garlic and stir-fry 30 seconds. Add curry powder and 1 or 2 tablespoons water. Cook 1 minute.
2. Add onion flakes and stir-fry briskly. Add tomato juice, bring to a simmer and add vegetables and fenugreek. Stir-fry 3 minutes.
3. Add yogurt, garam masala and chopped cilantro. Cook 2 to 3 minutes, adding a little water if necessary to prevent sticking.
4. Add salt and garnish with cilantro leaves and carrot.

Makes 2 servings.

Each serving contains:

Cal	Prot	Carb	Fib	Tot. Fat	Sat. Fat	Chol	Sodium
362	8g	38g	10g	23g	3g	2mg	334mg

Opposite: Balti Chicken, Broccoli, Lentils and Peas (page 44) served with Curry Yellow Raita (page 109)

BALTI CHICKEN, BROCCOLI, LENTILS AND PEAS

Here is a typical combination of balti ingredients. The mixture should include not only different tastes, but also different shapes, colors and textures.

4 tablespoons clarified butter or
   vegetable oil
1/2 teaspoon cumin seeds
1/2 teaspoon fennel seeds
1/4 teaspoon cardamom seeds
2 teaspoons minced garlic
1 teaspoon minced fresh ginger
1 tablespoon Homemade Curry
   Powder, page 6
1 tablespoon Garam Masala, page 5
6 tablespoons dried onion flakes
1/3 cup (80ml) tomato juice
1/4 cup (60ml) red wine or water

1/2 lb. (225g) boned, skinned
   chicken breasts, cubed
1 tablespoon chopped bell pepper
1 green chile pepper, chopped
1 teaspoon dried fenugreek leaves
2 tablespoons plain yogurt
1 tablespoon chopped cilantro
1/3 cup (85g) frozen broccoli,
   thawed
1/4 cup (60g) frozen peas, thawed
3-4 tablespoons cooked lentils
Salt to taste
Garnish—cilantro leaves

Each serving contains:

Cal	Prot	Carb	Fib	Tot. Fat	Sat. Fat	Chol	Sodium
522	31g	31g	8g	31g	17g	130mg	366mg

1. Heat half the butter or oil in wok or large skillet. Stir-fry seeds 20 seconds. Add garlic and ginger and cook 30 seconds longer. Add remaining butter or oil, curry powder and garam masala.
2. Add onion flakes and stir-fry briskly. Add tomato juice and red wine or water. Bring to a simmer and add chicken, peppers and fenugreek leaves.
3. Stir-fry 10 minutes, then add yogurt, chopped cilantro, broccoli, peas and lentils.
4. Continue cooking and stirring another 5 minutes, until chicken is done, adding more water if necessary to prevent sticking.
5. Add salt, garnish with cilantro leaves and serve.

Makes 2 servings.

Variation

Ground Meat Balti—Replace chicken with ground beef, lamb or pork. Omit broccoli, peas and lentils. Add 2 ounces (60g) cooked shrimp, 1/2 cup (130g) cooked chickpeas and 10 to 12 chopped spinach leaves.

Chapter Five

MEAT CURRIES

To cook a meat curry from scratch in under half an hour, cut the meat into 1/2-inch (1.25cm) cubes or thin slices, as in Chinese stir-fry style. Use only best-quality lean meat. It tastes better and requires the least preparation time. The following recipes give you a variety of meats cooked in a variety of ways.

SHEEK KEBAB—BURGER-STYLE

Serve these in buns, with salad and chutney. You've never had a better-tasting burger.

1 lb. (450g) extra-lean ground
  beef
2-3 cloves garlic, chopped
1 tablespoon chopped mint
2 tablespoons chopped cilantro
4 tablespoons dried onion flakes,
  crumbled
2 teaspoons Tandoori Curry
  Powder, page 7

1 teaspoon Garam Masala, page 5
1 teaspoon cumin seeds
1-2 green chile peppers, chopped
1/2 teaspoon salt
3 tablespoons clarified butter
  or oil

1. Combine all ingredients except butter or oil. Using your hands, mix together until well blended. Divide mixture into 4 patties.
2. Heat butter or oil in large skillet. Fry patties over medium heat, 5 minutes on each side, until done as desired.

Makes 2 servings.

Each serving contains:

Cal	Prot	Carb	Fib	Tot. Fat	Sat. Fat	Chol	Sodium
634	46g	14g	3g	44g	21g	200mg	808mg

STIR-FRIED SHASHLIK

This ancient Middle Eastern favorite is usually cooked on skewers. I have stir-fried it with great results. The trick is to cut the steak into very thin slices, which is easy to do if it is partially frozen. If you have the time, thread the ingredients onto bamboo skewers *after* cooking. Serve on a bed of rice with salad, lemon wedges and chutneys.

1 (10-oz. / 280g) boneless beef
   steak
2 tablespoons vegetable oil
1 teaspoon minced fresh garlic
1 teaspoon minced fresh ginger
1 tablespoon Homemade Curry
   Powder, page 6
1 tablespoon water
1/2 red bell pepper, cored, seeded
   and sliced

1/2 green bell pepper, cored,
   seeded and sliced
2 red chile peppers (optional)
1 small onion, sliced
Salt to taste
1 teaspoon Garam Masala, page 5
1/4 cup (60ml) dry sherry

1. Cut meat into thin slices (1-1/2 x 1 inch / 3.75 x 2.5cm).
2. Heat oil in wok or large skillet. Stir-fry garlic and ginger
   20 seconds. Add curry powder and water and cook 1 minute.
3. Add meat, peppers and onion and stir-fry 3 to 4 minutes.
4. Add salt, garam masala and sherry and continue cooking until
   meat is tender.

Makes 2 servings.

Each serving contains:

Cal	Prot	Carb	Fib	Tot. Fat	Sat. Fat	Chol	Sodium
413	35g	12g	4g	24g	5g	96mg	218mg

SPINACH AND BEEF (SAG GOSHT)

Sag means "spinach" and *gosht* means "meat." This dish is from the Punjab—the northwest corner of the Indian subcontinent, now straddled by Pakistan and India. Serve it with rice or, as the Punjabis do, with naan bread. Add a salad, lemon wedges and chutneys.

4 tablespoons clarified butter
1 teaspoon cumin seeds
1/2 teaspoon fennel seeds
2-3 cardamom pods
2-3 bay leaves
3 teaspoons minced garlic
1 teaspoon minced fresh ginger
1 tablespoon Homemade Curry Powder, page 6
Water
3/4 lb. (340g) lean stew beef, cut into 1/2-inch (1.25cm) cubes
5-6 green onions (leaves and bulbs), chopped

2/3 cup (160ml) onion soup, stock or water
1 tablespoon tomato purée
1 tablespoon ketchup
1 teaspoon dried fenugreek leaves
1 small bunch spinach, chopped
1 teaspoon chopped mint
1/4 teaspoon vinegar
1 tablespoon chopped cilantro
2 teaspoons Garam Masala, page 5
Salt to taste

Each serving contains:

Cal	Prot	Carb	Fib	Tot. Fat	Sat. Fat	Chol	Sodium
553	36g	16g	6g	40g	20g	171mg	945mg

1. Heat butter in wok or large skillet. Stir-fry spices 20 seconds. Add garlic and ginger and stir-fry 30 seconds. Add curry powder and briskly stir in, then add 1 to 2 tablespoons water.
2. Add meat and green onions, and stir-fry about 5 minutes. Add water as needed to simmer without sticking.
3. Add soup, stock or water, tomato purée, ketchup and fenugreek leaves. Simmer 5 minutes, stirring as necessary.
4. Add spinach, mint, vinegar, cilantro and garam masala. Simmer and stir 5 minutes, until meat is done. Add salt to taste. Remove and discard bay leaves.

Makes 2 servings.

SPICY RIBS

Ribs and chops are not traditional cuts of meat in India. However, they respond well to spicy treatment, as in Tandoori Lamb Chops, page 29. The spices are different in this recipe. Serve the ribs with rice and chutneys.

1 lb. (450g) lamb or pork ribs,
  bone in
6 tablespoons soy or sunflower oil
1/4 teaspoon vinegar
1 teaspoon minced fresh mint
1 teaspoon ground coriander
1 teaspoon ground cumin

1/2 teaspoon chili powder
2 teaspoons Homemade Curry
  Powder, page 6
2 teaspoons dried cilantro
1/2 teaspoon salt
Garnish—snipped chives

1. Preheat broiler, line broiler pan with foil, and put the rack over it.
2. With a sharp knife, cut small slashes into ribs.
3. Mix remaining ingredients, except chives, in large nonmetallic bowl.
4. Coat ribs thoroughly with mixture. Place on rack and broil 5 minutes.
5. Turn over ribs and baste with remaining mixture. Broil 5 minutes, until cooked.
6. Top with juices, if any, and garnish with chives.

Makes 2 servings.

Each serving contains:

Cal	Prot	Carb	Fib	Tot. Fat	Sat. Fat	Chol	Sodium
809	26g	3g	2g	77g	21g	116mg	631mg

SPICY SCALLOPS OF VEAL OR PORK

Both of these meats are wonderful pounded thin and coated with seasoned breadcrumbs. Serve with a fruit salad and Plain Boiled Rice, page 102, into which you have stirred a tablespoon or two of unsalted butter and some chili powder, or with Spicy Spaghetti or Noodles, page 13 (served hot).

2 veal or pork scallops, each 6 oz. (170g)	1 teaspoon snipped chives
2 large eggs	1 red chile pepper, minced
2 teaspoons Garam Masala, page 5	1/2 teaspoon salt
2 teaspoons finely chopped cilantro	1/3 cup (60g) breadcrumbs
	3 tablespoons butter

1. Pound meat until thin, if necessary, and wipe dry.
2. Beat eggs in a bowl; add remaining ingredients except breadcrumbs and butter.
3. Dip meat in egg mixture, then coat with breadcrumbs, pressing firmly.
4. Heat butter in large skillet and fry meat about 4 minutes per side.

Makes 2 servings.

Each serving contains:

				Tot.	Sat.		
Cal	Prot	Carb	Fib	Fat	Fat	Chol	Sodium
535	50g	18g	2g	47g	22g	416mg	1020mg

CHILE-AND-PEPPER STEAK

In this variation of a popular favorite, chile peppers and spices are incorporated into the steak. Fillet steak 1-1/4 inches (3.25cm) thick should be pan-fried 3 minutes on each side for rare, 4 to 6 minutes for medium and 6 to 10 minutes for well-done. Serve with a salad or with rice and a mix-in sauce from chapter 9.

1/2 teaspoon black peppercorns, crushed

1/2 teaspoon cumin seeds, roasted, page 2

1/4 teaspoon green peppercorns in brine, crushed

1/4 teaspoon coriander seeds, roasted, page 2, then crushed

1 tablespoon minced cilantro

1 green chile pepper, minced

1 teaspoon Garam Masala, page 5

1/4 teaspoon turmeric

2 boneless beef steaks, each about 6 oz. (170g)

2 tablespoons oil

1. Combine all ingredients except steaks and oil.
2. Coat both sides of meat with spice mixture.
3. Heat oil in skillet. Fry steaks until done as desired. To minimize burning of the coating, add a teaspoon of water as needed.

Makes 2 servings.

Each serving contains:

Cal	Prot	Carb	Fib	Tot. Fat	Sat. Fat	Chol	Sodium
397	40g	3g	1g	24g	6g	115mg	89mg

STIR-FRIED MEAT (JALFREZI)

The British in India developed a way to use leftover roasts. They called it *jalfrezi* (dry-fry). It can now mean a stir-fry of fresh ingredients, but this is the original "dry-fry" of leftover cooked meat.

2 tablespoons clarified butter
1 teaspoon cumin seeds
1/2 teaspoon mustard seed
1/2 teaspoon sesame seeds
1/2 teaspoon turmeric
1/4 teaspoon chili powder
2 teaspoons minced garlic
1 tablespoon Homemade Curry Powder, page 6
1/3 cup (80ml) tomato juice
6 tablespoons dried onion flakes
2 tablespoons butter

1 tablespoon prawn balichow
1/4 cup (60g) sliced carrot
2 tablespoons chopped bell pepper
1-2 green chile peppers, chopped
1 teaspoon dried cilantro
2-3 green onions (leaves and bulbs), chopped
1/4 cup (60ml) cream
1-1/4 cups (280g) cooked meat, cubed
1-2 teaspoons Garam Masala, page 5
Salt to taste

1. Heat butter in wok or large skillet. Stir-fry spices 20 seconds, then add garlic and stir-fry 20 seconds. Add curry powder and stir-fry 30 seconds.
2. Add 2 to 3 tablespoons tomato juice and onion flakes and stir-fry briskly 30 seconds. Add remaining tomato juice and butter. When sizzling, add prawn balichow, carrot, peppers, cilantro and green onions.
3. Stir-fry 4 minutes, then add cream, meat and garam masala and simmer 5 minutes. Add salt and serve.

Makes 2 servings.

Each serving contains:

Cal	Prot	Carb	Fib	Tot. Fat	Sat. Fat	Chol	Sodium
649	38g	24g	7g	46g	25g	199mg	520mg

KEEMA WITH KIDNEY BEANS

This ground-meat curry comes originally from Kashmir and uses ginger (plenty of it), chile peppers (as many as you dare) and red kidney beans. Serve with rice or bread.

2 tablespoons vegetable oil
3/4 lb. (340g) ground beef, lamb
*   or pork*
2 tablespoons clarified butter
2 teaspoons Garam Masala, page 5
1 teaspoon ground coriander
1/2 teaspoon ground cumin
1/2 teaspoon chili powder (or
*   more)*
2 teaspoons minced garlic

1 tablespoon minced fresh ginger
1-4 red chile peppers, sliced
3-4 green onions (leaves and
*   bulbs), chopped*
3-4 canned plum tomatoes
1 tablespoon ketchup
1/3 cup (85g) canned red kidney
*   beans, drained and rinsed*
1 tablespoon chopped cilantro
Salt to taste

1. Heat oil in saucepan. Add ground meat and cook 20 minutes, stirring occasionally. Add water by spoonfuls, if necessary.
2. Meanwhile, heat butter in wok or large skillet. Stir-fry spices 30 seconds. Add garlic and stir-fry 30 seconds. Add ginger, chile peppers and green onions and cook 1 minute.
3. Transfer ground meat to the wok, mixing well. Add tomatoes and ketchup and simmer 5 minutes.
4. Add kidney beans and cilantro. Cook 5 minutes, adding a little water if necessary. Add salt to taste.

Makes 2 servings.

Each serving contains:

Cal	Prot	Carb	Fib	Tot. Fat	Sat. Fat	Chol	Sodium
699	40g	30g	9g	48g	18g	150mg	358mg

Chapter Six

POULTRY CURRIES

Chicken is a gift for the quick-after-work curry cook. It takes less than 15 minutes to cook, even in quite large chunks. Always use skinless poultry in curry dishes and cook thoroughly at a high temperature. Before serving, cut the largest piece of chicken in half to check that there is no uncooked meat in the center.

CHICKEN KEBAB—BURGER STYLE

Chicken is a welcome alternative to red meat for burgers. I use dark chicken meat or turkey leg meat and grind it in a food processor. Serve the burgers in buns, with salad and chutneys.

1 lb. (450g) ground chicken
  or turkey
2-3 cloves garlic, chopped
1 tablespoon chopped mint
2 tablespoons chopped cilantro
4 tablespoons dried onion flakes,
  crumbled
2 teaspoons Tandoori Curry
  Powder, page 7

1 teaspoon Garam Masala, page 5
1 teaspoon cumin seeds
1-2 green chile peppers, chopped
  (optional)
1/2 teaspoon salt
3 tablespoons clarified butter

1. Combine all ingredients except clarified butter.
2. Using your hands, mix together until well blended. Shape into 4 burgers.
3. Heat butter in large skillet. Fry burgers over medium heat at least 5 minutes on each side, until done as desired.

Makes 2 servings.

Each serving contains:

Cal	Prot	Carb	Fib	Tot. Fat	Sat. Fat	Chol	Sodium
296	23g	5g	1g	21g	9g	107mg	426mg

STIR-FRIED CHICKEN AND PEPPERS (HASINA)

This recipe, like Shashlik, page 49, originated in the Middle East. It combines chicken with colorful red and green peppers. Serve on a bed of rice with a green salad, melon slices, lemon wedges and chutneys.

10 oz. (280g) boned, skinned
   chicken breasts
1/2 red bell pepper, cored and
   seeded
1/2 green bell pepper, cored and
   seeded
1 small onion
2 tablespoons vegetable oil
1 teaspoon minced garlic

1 teaspoon minced fresh ginger
1 tablespoon Homemade Curry
   Powder, page 6
1 tablespoon water
2 red chile peppers, chopped
1 teaspoon Garam Masala, page 5
4 tablespoons dry sherry
Salt to taste

1. Cut chicken into 1-inch (2.5cm) cubes. Cut peppers and onion into 1-inch (2.5cm) squares.
2. Heat oil in wok or large skillet. Stir-fry garlic and ginger 20 seconds. Add curry powder and water and stir-fry 1 minute.
3. Add chicken and stir-fry 6 to 8 minutes.
4. Add peppers, onion, garam masala and sherry and cook 6 to 10 minutes, until chicken is tender. Add salt to taste.

Makes 2 servings.

Each serving contains:

Cal	Prot	Carb	Fib	Tot. Fat	Sat. Fat	Chol	Sodium
366	32g	16g	5g	19g	3g	78mg	218mg

CHICKEN JALFREZI

As mentioned on page 55, *jalfrezi* was one of the ways in which the Raj used leftovers. It can also be a stir-fry of fresh ingredients. This dish adds lovely, yellow-golden curry spices, herbs and a little chile flavor. Serve with plain rice and chutneys.

3 tablespoons clarified butter
1 teaspoon cumin seeds
1 teaspoon sesame seeds
1/2 teaspoon turmeric
2-4 cloves garlic, chopped
1 tablespoon chopped fresh ginger
1 tablespoon Homemade Curry
   Powder, page 6
1-2 tablespoons water
3/4 lb. (340g) boned, skinned
   chicken breasts, cubed
4 tablespoons dried onion flakes
1 tablespoon chopped bell pepper

1-2 green chile peppers, chopped
2-3 tomatoes, quartered
1 oz. (30g) creamed coconut,
   chopped, page 4
1 teaspoon dried cilantro
1 tablespoon brinjal (eggplant)
   pickle, chopped (optional)
2 teaspoons chopped cilantro
   and/or 2 teaspoons chopped
   mint
1 teaspoon Garam Masala, page 5
Salt to taste

Each serving contains:

Cal	Prot	Carb	Fib	Tot. Fat	Sat. Fat	Chol	Sodium
496	39g	26g	7g	29g	16g	143mg	249mg

1. Heat butter in wok or large skillet. Stir-fry seeds and turmeric 20 seconds. Add garlic and ginger and stir-fry 30 seconds. Add curry powder and water and cook another minute.
2. Add chicken pieces, onion flakes and peppers and stir-fry 3 to 4 minutes, adding spoonfuls of water as needed.
3. Lower heat, add tomatoes, coconut, dried cilantro and pickle, if using. Cook 10 minutes, stirring occasionally and adding water as needed.
4. Add chopped cilantro and/or mint, garam masala and salt.

Makes 2 servings.

Variation

Cumin Chicken—Omit turmeric and chopped mint. Add 2 teaspoons ground cumin and 1 tablespoon mango chutney and increase chopped cilantro to 1 tablespoon. Garnish with 2 teaspoons roasted cumin seeds, page 2.

BUTTER CHICKEN

This rich dish goes under the name *Makhani Chicken* in India, where it uses white buffalo butter. I've substituted ordinary butter and used minimal spicing. To prevent overpowering its unique caramelized flavors, I recommend that you serve it with Plain Boiled Rice, page 102, and Quick Tasty Dhal, page 85.

2 tablespoons clarified butter
1 tablespoon Bengali Five-Spice
   Mixture, page 7
2 teaspoons paprika
1/2 teaspoon chili powder
2-4 cloves garlic, chopped
2-3 tablespoons butter
1 teaspoon Tandoori Curry
   Powder, page 7
3/4 lb. (340g) boned, skinned
   chicken breasts, cubed

4 tablespoons dried onion flakes
2 tablespoons chopped bell pepper
1 red chile pepper, chopped
3-4 tomatoes, quartered
1 tablespoon tomato purée
1 tablespoon chopped mango
   chutney
2 teaspoons chopped cilantro
2 teaspoons chopped fresh basil
1 teaspoon Garam Masala, page 5
Salt to taste

1. Heat butter in wok or large skillet. Stir-fry five-spice mixture, paprika and chili powder 20 seconds. Add garlic and stir-fry 30 seconds. Add butter and curry powder.
2. Add chicken pieces, onion flakes and peppers and stir-fry 3 to 4 minutes, adding water if needed.
3. Lower heat, add tomatoes, tomato purée and chutney and cook 10 minutes, stirring occasionally and adding water as needed.
4. Add cilantro, basil, garam masala and salt.

Makes 2 servings.

Each serving contains:

Cal	Prot	Carb	Fib	Tot. Fat	Sat. Fat	Chol	Sodium
581	39g	29g	6g	36g	20g	173mg	550mg

CHILE CHICKEN

Scientists have written pages explaining why people enjoy hot food. But save that for later, there's no time now! Because in 20 minutes you could be enjoying this uncompromisingly chile-hot dish. Serve with avocado slices and a green salad.

3 tablespoons vegetable oil
1 teaspoon cumin seeds
1/2 teaspoon coriander seeds
1/2 teaspoon mustard seeds
1 teaspoon hot chili powder
1 tablespoon minced garlic
1 tablespoon Homemade Curry
  Powder, page 6
3/4 lb. (340g) boned, skinned
  chicken, cubed
4 tablespoons dried onion flakes
1 tablespoon bell pepper, chopped

2-4 green chile peppers, chopped
2-3 canned tomatoes, chopped
1/4 teaspoon vinegar
1 oz. (30g) creamed coconut,
  chopped, page 4
1-2 tablespoons chili pickle
  (optional)
1 tablespoon chopped cilantro
2 tablespoons chopped mint
1 teaspoon Garam Masala, page 5
Salt to taste

1. Heat oil in wok or large skillet. Stir-fry seeds and chili powder 20 seconds. Add garlic and stir-fry 30 seconds. Add curry powder and 1 to 2 tablespoons water and cook 1 minute.
2. Add chicken pieces, onion flakes and peppers and stir-fry 3 to 4 minutes, adding water if needed.
3. Lower the heat, add tomatoes, vinegar, creamed coconut and chili pickle, if using. Cook 10 minutes, stirring occasionally and adding water as needed.
4. Add cilantro, mint, garam masala and salt.

Makes 2 servings.

Each serving contains:

Cal	Prot	Carb	Fib	Tot. Fat	Sat. Fat	Chol	Sodium
527	40g	30g	8g	30g	7g	94mg	264mg

CHICKEN DOPIAZA

Do means "two," *piaza* means "onion." This recipe uses onions in three different ways plus canned onion soup. The result is really oniony—and totally delicious.

2 tablespoons sunflower oil
1 small cinnamon stick
1 star anise
2 cardamom pods, crushed
4-6 cloves
1 tablespoon Homemade Curry
Powder, page 6
1/2 cup (115g) chopped onions
4 small pickling onions or
shallots, peeled and halved
2-3 bay leaves

1 cup (250ml) canned onion soup
4 skinless chicken drumsticks,
each about 4 oz. (115g)
2-3 green onions (leaves and
bulbs), cut in strips lengthwise
1 dried red chile pepper, chopped
1-1/2 teaspoons Garam Masala,
page 5
Salt to taste

1. Preheat oven to 375F (190C). Heat oil in casserole dish.
2. Sauté cinnamon, star anise, cardamom and cloves 10 seconds.
3. Add curry powder and stir-fry 30 seconds. Add chopped onion and stir-fry on low heat 5 minutes.
4. Add pickling onions, bay leaves, onion soup and drumsticks. Increase heat and bring to a simmer.
5. Transfer to oven. After 15 minutes add green onions, red chile pepper and garam masala. Bake another 15 minutes. Check that chicken is cooked through, then add salt. Remove and discard bay leaves and other whole spices.

Makes 2 servings.

Each serving contains:

Cal	Prot	Carb	Fib	Tot. Fat	Sat. Fat	Chol	Sodium
539	54g	28g	6g	25g	4g	175mg	1379mg

GROUND CHICKEN OR TURKEY CURRY

This dish cooks in about 12 minutes. Serve it with bread and a salad unless you have some rice already cooked in the refrigerator.

3 tablespoons clarified butter
1 teaspoon cumin seeds
1/2 teaspoon coriander seeds
1/2 teaspoon fennel seeds
1/4 teaspoon celery seeds
1/4 teaspoon cardamom seeds
1 teaspoon minced garlic
2 teaspoons Homemade Curry Powder, page 6
1/2 lb. (225g) ground chicken or turkey
5-6 green onions (leaves and bulbs), chopped

2 tablespoons chopped bell pepper
1-2 red chile peppers, chopped
3-4 cherry tomatoes, quartered
2/3 cup (160ml) canned cream of mushroom soup
8-10 fresh button mushrooms, quartered
1 teaspoon prepared mustard
1 teaspoon horseradish sauce
2 tablespoons chopped cilantro
1 teaspoon Garam Masala, page 5
Salt to taste

1. Heat butter in wok or large skillet. Stir-fry seeds 20 seconds. Add garlic and stir-fry 30 seconds longer. Stir in curry powder and 1 to 2 tablespoons of water, if needed to prevent burning.
2. Add ground meat and stir 1 to 2 minutes, then mix in green onions, peppers and tomatoes. When sizzling, add soup 1 tablespoon at a time, mixing well after each addition.
3. The mixture should be creamy in texture, but sizzling nicely. Add remaining ingredients except salt and simmer 5 minutes. Add salt to taste and serve.

Makes 2 servings.

Each serving contains:

Cal	Prot	Carb	Fib	Tot. Fat	Sat. Fat	Chol	Sodium
533	27g	23g	5g	38g	17g	134mg	970mg

Chapter Seven

FISH AND SEAFOOD CURRIES

In my opinion, some of India's best dishes are the fish and shellfish curries. I wish we encountered more of them in restaurants. The seven recipes here are quite different in character. Four are authentic recipes from India and Bangladesh. Creamy Shrimp Kofta is my own invention. It's very tasty and, like all the recipes in this chapter, very quick to cook.

It is worth making the effort to track down the huge tiger prawns used in Cumin Tiger Prawns. Lobster and Shrimp Jalfrezi is expensive, but worth having on that special occasion.

Either shrimp or prawns may be used in these recipes. If prawn balichow is not available, substitute chopped shrimp or shrimp paste.

CUMIN TIGER PRAWNS

Buy uncooked frozen tiger prawns without heads but with shells and tails. Native to the Bay of Bengal, they are called *tiger prawns* because of the black stripes on their backs. Thaw in a covered bowl in the refrigerator. Serve with lime wedges, sliced tomatoes and Indian bread.

1/2 lb. (225g) unshelled tiger
   prawns
Juice of 2 limes
2 tablespoons butter
2 teaspoons cumin seeds
1/2 teaspoon turmeric
1 teaspoon Homemade Curry
   Powder, page 6

2 cloves garlic, finely chopped
2-3 green onions (leaves and
   bulbs), finely chopped
Salt to taste
Garnishes—snipped chives, dried
   coconut, chili powder

1. Remove shell, legs and tails from prawns. Cut a slit down the back and remove the vein. Rinse and pat dry with a paper towel, then rub with lime juice.
2. Heat butter in wok or large skillet. Stir-fry cumin seeds 20 seconds. Add turmeric and curry powder; stir-fry 20 seconds. Add garlic and green onions. Stir-fry 2 to 3 minutes.
3. Add prawns; cook 12 minutes, maintaining a gentle sizzle without burning spices. Add teaspoonfuls of water to prevent sticking.
4. When prawns are ready their centers should be an even bright white. Cut one in half to check.
5. Salt to taste, garnish and serve.

Makes 2 servings.

Each serving contains:

Cal	Prot	Carb	Fib	Tot. Fat	Sat. Fat	Chol	Sodium
263	24g	6g	3g	16g	10g	31mg	270mg

CREAMY SHRIMP KOFTA

This recipe combines frozen shrimp and a rich curry sauce, merging East and West. The amounts of soup and cream or milk will vary according to the creaminess or thickness of the soup.

4 tablespoons butter
1 teaspoon sesame seeds
1/2 teaspoon celery seeds
1/2 teaspoon nigella (black seeds)
1/2 teaspoon turmeric
2 teaspoons minced garlic
3-4 green onions (bulbs and
    leaves), chopped
2 teaspoons Homemade Curry
    Powder, page 6
1 teaspoon Tandoori Curry
    Powder, page 7

3/4 cup (185ml) canned
    vichyssoise
1 green chile pepper, sliced
    (optional)
2-3 tomatoes, quartered
1 tablespoon prawn balichow
1/2 teaspoon dried cilantro
Cream or milk
3 tablespoons vegetable oil
1 lb. (450g) frozen deveined
    shrimp
Salt to taste

1. Heat butter in wok or large skillet. Stir-fry seeds 10 seconds. Add turmeric and cook 10 seconds. Add garlic and stir-fry 30 seconds. Add green onions and cook 2 minutes, then add curry powders.
2. Add soup a spoonful at a time over a 3-minute period.
3. Add chile pepper, if using, tomatoes, prawn balichow, cilantro and enough cream or milk to simmer gently without sticking.
4. Meanwhile, heat oil in a flat skillet. Add frozen shrimp 3 or 4 at a time, stirring constantly for the 5 minutes it takes to cook them.
5. Mix shrimp with sauce, add salt and serve at once.

Makes 2 servings.

Each serving contains:

Cal	Prot	Carb	Fib	Tot. Fat	Sat. Fat	Chol	Sodium
746	41g	23g	4g	56g	23g	413mg	1246mg

LOBSTER AND SHRIMP JALFREZI

Occasionally we all want to cook something special, to mark a birthday or anniversary—or just to be different. And because such dates often fall on workdays, here is a wonderful recipe that takes just minutes to cook.

2-3 tablespoons clarified butter
1/2 teaspoon fennel seeds
1/2 teaspoon sesame seeds
1/2 teaspoon white poppy seeds
1/4 teaspoon turmeric
2-3 cloves garlic, chopped
1 tablespoon Homemade Curry
  Powder, page 6
1/3 cup (80ml) milk
4 tablespoons toasted onion flakes

1/2 lb. (225g) cooked lobster
  meat
1 can (4-oz. / 115g) shrimp,
  drained
1/3 cup (80ml) cream
1 tablespoon prawn balichow
1 tablespoon chopped cilantro
2 teaspoons ground almonds
1 teaspoon Garam Masala, page 5
Salt to taste

1. Heat clarified butter in wok or large skillet. Stir-fry seeds and turmeric 10 seconds, add garlic and stir-fry 30 seconds. Add curry powder and 1 to 2 tablespoons milk and cook 3 to 4 minutes.
2. Add onion flakes, then add remaining milk a spoonful at a time, stirring constantly.
3. Add lobster, shrimp and half the cream and stir-fry 2 to 3 minutes. Add prawn balichow, cilantro, almonds, garam masala and remaining cream. If mixture is dry, add water until texture is creamy.
4. Simmer 3 to 4 minutes, add salt and serve.

Makes 2 servings.

Each serving contains:

Cal	Prot	Carb	Fib	Tot. Fat	Sat. Fat	Chol	Sodium
576	42g	21g	4g	37g	18g	258mg	707mg

KERALA CRAB CURRY

Kerala is at the southernmost tip of India. The food is lighter than that of the north and often blended with fruit of the palm—coconut. Crabmeat sings with such spicing. Serve with rice and chutneys.

3 tablespoons sesame or soy oil
1 teaspoon mustard seeds
1 teaspoon sesame seeds
1/4 teaspoon celery seeds
1/2 teaspoon crushed red pepper
1/4 teaspoon turmeric
1/2 teaspoon ground coriander
1/2 teaspoon chili powder
2-4 cloves garlic, chopped
5-6 green onions (leaves and
  bulbs), chopped
1-2 fresh green chile peppers,
  chopped

3/4 cup (185ml) water
10-12 curry leaves, dried or fresh
  (optional)
1 oz. (30g) creamed coconut,
  chopped, page 4
2 tablespoons coconut-milk powder
1 tablespoon prawn balichow
1 tablespoon chopped bell pepper
12 oz. (340g) crabmeat
Salt to taste
Garnish—2 limes, quartered

1. Heat oil in wok or large skillet. Stir-fry seeds and spices 10 seconds. Add garlic and stir-fry 10 seconds, then add green onions and chile peppers and cook 2 to 3 minutes. Don't let it stick.
2. Add water and curry leaves, if using, and bring to a simmer. Stir in creamed coconut and coconut-milk powder.
3. Add prawn balichow, bell pepper and crabmeat. Add more water if necessary to keep mixture creamy.
4. Stir-fry 5 minutes, then add salt. Garnish with lime quarters.

Makes 2 servings.

Each serving contains:

Cal	Prot	Carb	Fib	Tot. Fat	Sat. Fat	Chol	Sodium
893	43g	19g	5g	76g	49g	120mg	781mg

GOAN SHRIMP CURRY

Goa is a small district on the western coast of India. Goans love the tart taste of vinegar and the piquancy of red chiles blended with warm spices and cashews and laced with wine.

1 tablespoon vinegar
1 teaspoon chili powder
1/2 teaspoon paprika
1/2 teaspoon ground coriander
1/2 teaspoon dried fenugreek
4 tablespoons soy or sunflower oil
1/2 teaspoon cumin seeds
1/2 teaspoon coriander seeds
1/2 teaspoon crushed red pepper
2 teaspoons minced garlic
1 teaspoon minced fresh ginger

4 tablespoons toasted onion flakes
12 oz. (340g) medium-size
  shrimp, cooked and shelled
1 teaspoon tomato purée
2 tablespoons coconut-milk powder
1 tablespoon chopped cilantro
1-2 fresh red chile peppers, sliced
12 cashews, finely chopped or
  coarsely ground
1/2 cup (125ml) port or Madeira
Salt to taste

1. In a nonmetallic bowl, combine vinegar, chili powder, paprika, coriander and fenugreek. Add water to make mixture pourable.
2. Heat oil in wok or large skillet. Stir-fry seeds and crushed red pepper 10 seconds. Add spice mixture (it will hiss and sputter) and stir-fry 1 minute. Add garlic and ginger and stir-fry 1 minute.
3. Add onion flakes. When they have absorbed the liquid in the pan (which happens quickly), add enough water to stop the sizzling.
4. Stir in shrimp, tomato purée, coconut-milk powder, cilantro, fresh chiles and cashews. Cook 3 minutes.
5. Add a little water to keep mixture from sticking. Stir-fry 2 to 3 minutes, then add port or Madeira and salt. Heat and serve.

Makes 2 servings.

Each serving contains:

Cal	Prot	Carb	Fib	Tot. Fat	Sat. Fat	Chol	Sodium
1009	31g	34g	5g	87g	49g	202mg	571mg

BANGLADESHI FISH (MACH GHOL)

Bangladeshi food is very different from Indian food. Fish, bones and all, is important to Bangladeshis. Here I recreate the divine subtle tastes of their food using *panch phoran* (Bengali five-spice mixture). However, I have omitted the bones.

2 tablespoons soy or sunflower oil
1 teaspoon white poppy seeds
1 teaspoon Bengali Five-Spice
   Mixture, page 7
1 teaspoon Dijon-style mustard
1/4 teaspoon turmeric
1 green chile pepper, minced
2-4 cloves garlic, chopped
3-4 green onions (leaves and
   bulbs), chopped

1 cup (250ml) water
2 fish fillets, each 8 oz. (225g)
1 tablespoon dried coconut
2 tablespoons coconut-milk
   powder
1 tablespoon mango pickle,
   minced
1 tablespoon chopped cilantro
Salt to taste

1. Heat oil in wok or large skillet. Stir-fry seeds and five-spice mixture 10 seconds. Add mustard, turmeric and chile pepper and continue stir-frying 30 seconds. Add garlic and green onions and cook 2 to 3 minutes.
2. Add water and bring to a simmer. Add fish and simmer 5 minutes, stirring gently from time to time.
3. Add remaining ingredients except salt.
4. Simmer 5 minutes until fish is cooked. Add salt and serve.

Makes 2 servings.

Each serving contains:

Cal	Prot	Carb	Fib	Tot. Fat	Sat. Fat	Chol	Sodium
831	49g	12g	4g	69g	47g	109mg	804mg

MALABAR FISH CURRY

The Malabar coast is in southwestern India, where fishing is a major industry. Here flat fish is poached in coconut milk colored pale yellow by the addition of turmeric and made savory with South Indian spices and lime pickle.

2 tablespoons sesame oil
1/2 teaspoon turmeric
1 teaspoon mustard seeds
1/2 teaspoon coriander seeds
1/2 teaspoon cumin seeds
3/4 cup (85g) finely sliced onion
1 tablespoon minced lime pickle
1 teaspoon dry mustard

1-3/4 cups (440ml) coconut milk
10-12 curry leaves, fresh or dried
   (optional)
2 lemon sole fillets, each
   about 8 oz. (225g)
Salt to taste
Garnishes—4-6 lime wedges,
   freshly ground black pepper

1. Heat oil in wok or large skillet. Stir-fry turmeric 10 seconds. Add seeds and stir-fry 30 seconds.
2. Add onion and cook 3 to 4 minutes.
3. Add lime pickle, mustard, coconut milk and curry leaves, if using. Bring to a simmer, add fish and simmer 10 to 15 minutes, until cooked. Add salt. Serve with lime wedges and black pepper.

Makes 2 servings.

Each serving contains:

Cal	Prot	Carb	Fib	Tot. Fat	Sat. Fat	Chol	Sodium
755	47g	10g	3g	60g	40g	109mg	664mg

Opposite: Goan Shrimp Curry (page 72) served with Quick Tasty Dhal
(page 85) and Pappadums (page 20)

Chapter Eight

VEGETABLE AND LENTIL DISHES

Nothing does vegetables more proud than the spices of India. Because most of us like our vegetable curries as side dishes, these ten recipes have been portioned as accompaniments. Serve with a main-course dish from another chapter, together with rice and/or bread. If you want an all-vegetarian meal, double the quantities or serve two or three of these dishes with rice and/or bread.

Opposite: Mushroom Bhaji (page 79) served with Pea Pullao Rice (page 103) and Muglai Sauce (page 94)

VEGETABLE BHUNA BHAJI

Any vegetable is known as a *bhaji* when it is curried. And *bhuna* is a style of cooking. To create this dish you can use any vegetables you want. My choices here are carrots, peas, green beans and corn (or frozen mixed vegetables) with celery.

3 tablespoons soy or sunflower oil
2 teaspoons Homemade Curry Powder, page 6
2 teaspoons minced garlic
2-3 tablespoons water
2-3 green onions (leaves and bulbs), chopped
1 tablespoon chopped bell pepper
2 teaspoons chopped brinjal (eggplant) pickle

1 teaspoon chopped mango pickle
1 teaspoon tomato purée
1/2 teaspoon horseradish sauce
1/2 pkg. (10-oz. / 280g) frozen mixed vegetables, thawed
1 stalk celery, chopped
2 teaspoons chopped cilantro
1/2 teaspoon Garam Masala, page 5
Salt to taste

1. Heat oil in wok or large skillet. Stir-fry curry powder 30 seconds. Add garlic and cook 30 seconds. Add water, green onions and pepper. Stir-fry 3 minutes.
2. Mix in pickles, tomato purée and horseradish sauce, then add vegetables, celery, cilantro and garam masala. Stir-fry until mixture sizzles. Add enough water to create desired consistency and simmer 3 to 4 minutes. Add salt to taste and serve.

Makes 2 servings.

Each serving contains:

Cal	Prot	Carb	Fib	Tot. Fat	Sat. Fat	Chol	Sodium
247	3g	14g	6g	22g	3g	1mg	359mg

CURRIED RATATOUILLE
(VEGETABLE JALFREZI BHAJI)

The eggplant, tomato, zucchini and onion in the canned ratatouille make it ideal for a jalfrezi-style stir-fry.

2 tablespoons soy or sunflower oil
1/2 teaspoon cumin seeds
1/2 teaspoon mustard seeds
1 teaspoon chopped garlic
2 teaspoons Homemade Curry
  Powder, page 6
4 tablespoons toasted onion flakes

1 can (8-oz. / 225g) ratatouille
1 teaspoon chopped fresh ginger
1 teaspoon chopped brinjal
  (eggplant) pickle
2 teaspoons chopped cilantro
1/2 teaspoon Garam Masala, page 5
Salt to taste

1. Heat oil in wok or large skillet. Stir-fry seeds and garlic 30 seconds. Add curry powder and stir-fry 30 seconds.
2. Add onion flakes. When they are sizzling, add remaining ingredients. Serve as soon as dish is hot.

Makes 2 servings.

Each serving contains:

Cal	Prot	Carb	Fib	Tot. Fat	Sat. Fat	Chol	Sodium
188	2g	16g	4g	15g	2g	0mg	162mg

INDONESIAN VEGETABLE CURRY

In this time-saving dish I use fresh mixed stir-fry vegetables. These usually include baby corn, bamboo shoots, bean sprouts, carrots, peppers and onions. Instead of turning them into a Chinese dish, I have created an Indonesian curry.

2 tablespoons sesame or vegetable oil
1/4 teaspoon fennel seeds
1/4 teaspoon sesame seeds
3-4 cloves, crushed
1/2 teaspoon Homemade Curry Powder, page 6
1/4 teaspoon ground cinnamon
1/4 teaspoon turmeric
2-3 cloves garlic, sliced
1-inch (2.5cm) piece fresh ginger, sliced

8 oz. (225g) prepared stir-fry vegetables
1/2 cup (125ml) coconut milk
1/2 teaspoon soy sauce
1/2 teaspoon hoisin sauce
1/2 teaspoon tomato purée
1 tablespoon peanut butter (optional)
1 teaspoon brinjal (eggplant) pickle (optional)
Salt to taste

1. Heat oil in wok or large skillet. Stir-fry seeds and spices 20 seconds. Add garlic and ginger and stir-fry 1 minute.
2. Add vegetables and mix in quickly. Stir-fry 1 minute, then add remaining ingredients.
3. Stir-fry 3 to 4 minutes until hot.

Makes 2 servings.

Each serving contains:

Cal	Prot	Carb	Fib	Tot. Fat	Sat. Fat	Chol	Sodium
305	5g	18g	7g	26g	13g	0mg	321mg

MUSHROOM BHAJI

Use any combination of wild and cultivated mushrooms to add zest to this recipe. The minimal cooking time ensures that the mushrooms remain crisp and full of flavor.

1/2 lb. (225g) mushrooms
2 tablespoons butter
1/2 teaspoon cumin seeds
1 teaspoon minced garlic
1 tablespoon chopped bell pepper
1 green chile pepper, shredded
3-4 green onions (leaves and
bulbs), finely chopped

1 tablespoon mint
1-1/2 teaspoons Homemade Curry
Powder, page 6
1/4 cup (60ml) water
2 teaspoons coconut-milk powder
1 teaspoon Garam Masala, page 5
Salt to taste

1. Clean mushrooms with a damp paper towel. Chop or slice them.
2. Heat butter in wok or large skillet. Stir-fry cumin seeds 10 seconds. Add garlic and peppers and stir-fry 1 minute.
3. Add green onions and mint and cook 2 to 3 minutes. Stir in curry powder and water.
4. Add mushrooms and stir quickly to coat evenly. Lower heat and simmer at least 3 minutes.
5. Add coconut-milk powder, garam masala and salt. Simmer 1 minute and serve.

Makes 2 servings.

Each serving contains:

Cal	Prot	Carb	Fib	Tot. Fat	Sat. Fat	Chol	Sodium
306	5g	13g	4g	29g	22g	31mg	273mg

COTTAGE CHEESE AND PEA CURRY

The Indian cheese *paneer* is time-consuming to make, but nutritionally good as well as something quite different on the table. Here I have substituted cottage cheese for the paneer in the famous Indian dish, *Mattar Paneer.*

2 tablespoons butter
1/2 teaspoon cumin seeds
1/4 teaspoon coriander seeds
1/4 teaspoon turmeric
2-3 cloves garlic, chopped
1 teaspoon Homemade Curry
   Powder, page 6

2-3 green onion bulbs, chopped
1/2 cup (115g) frozen peas
2 teaspoons chopped cilantro
2 teaspoons chopped mint
1 teaspoon Garam Masala, page 5
1/2 cup (115g) cottage cheese
Salt to taste

1. Heat butter in wok or large skillet. Stir-fry seeds and turmeric 20 seconds. Add garlic and curry powder and cook 30 seconds.
2. Add green onions and frozen peas and stir-fry 3 minutes, until peas are thawed.
3. Stir in cilantro, mint and garam masala and then add cottage cheese and salt to taste.

Makes 2 servings.

Each serving contains:

Cal	Prot	Carb	Fib	Tot. Fat	Sat. Fat	Chol	Sodium
205	10g	11g	4g	15g	9g	39mg	536mg

POTATO, CAULIFLOWER AND SPINACH CURRY
(ALOO GHOBI SAG)

Potato (*aloo*), cauliflower (*ghobi*) and spinach (*sag*) combine to make a classic curry dish from northern India and Pakistan.

1/2 cup (85g) cauliflower florets
2 tablespoons clarified butter
1/2 teaspoon fennel seeds
1/4 teaspoon coriander seeds
1 teaspoon chopped garlic
1 teaspoon Homemade Curry
  Powder, page 6
3 tablespoons plain yogurt
1 teaspoon dried fenugreek leaves

1 small bunch (175g) fresh
  spinach, chopped, or
  1 10-oz. pkg. frozen
  chopped spinach, thawed
1 tablespoon butter
6-8 small new potatoes, boiled
1 tablespoon chopped cilantro
1 teaspoon Garam Masala, page 5
Salt to taste

1. Blanch cauliflower in boiling water or in the microwave.
2. Heat clarified butter in wok or large skillet. Stir-fry seeds 30 seconds. Add garlic and curry powder and stir-fry 1 minute.
3. Add yogurt, fenugreek, spinach and butter and stir-fry 2 to 3 minutes until spinach has softened.
4. Add remaining ingredients and enough water to prevent sticking.
5. When heated through, salt to taste and serve.

Makes 2 servings.

Variation
Substitute broccoli for cauliflower.

Each serving contains:

Cal	Prot	Carb	Fib	Tot. Fat	Sat. Fat	Chol	Sodium
446	9g	62g	7g	20g	12g	50mg	301mg

BOMBAY POTATOES

Nothing improves potatoes more than a tasty curry gravy. This combination is so popular that Indian restaurants have devised a name for it—*Bombay Potatoes*. The quickest way to make the dish is to reheat cooked potatoes. Canned ones can also be used.

3 tablespoons clarified butter
2 teaspoons minced garlic
1 teaspoon Homemade Curry
  Powder, page 6
4 tablespoons toasted onion flakes
1/4 cup (60ml) milk
1 teaspoon tomato purée
2 teaspoons chopped bell pepper

1/2-1 teaspoon chopped chile
  pepper
1 teaspoon Garam Masala, page 5
10-12 small new potatoes, boiled
2 tablespoons plain yogurt
1-2 teaspoons chopped cilantro
Salt to taste

1. Heat butter in wok or large skillet. Stir-fry garlic and curry powder 1 to 2 minutes. Mix in onion flakes and milk. Stir-fry 1 minute.
2. Mix in tomato purée, peppers and garam masala; add potatoes and stir-fry 2 to 3 minutes.
3. Add yogurt and cilantro and stir-fry 2 minutes. Add salt to taste and serve.

Makes 2 servings.

Each serving contains:

Cal	Prot	Carb	Fib	Tot. Fat	Sat. Fat	Chol	Sodium
577	10g	92g	7g	21g	13g	52mg	195mg

LENTIL CURRY (MADRASI SAMBAR)

Cooks in southern India combine vegetables, lentils and chile peppers in the classic dish *sambar*. My quick version is based on a recipe from Madras, its typical tart flavor produced by lime pickle. Serve with a main-course curry, plain rice and chutneys.

1 cup (250ml) vegetable stock
   or water
1/4 cup (60g) split red lentils
2 teaspoons dried coconut
1 red chile pepper
10-12 curry leaves, fresh or dried
   (optional)
2 tablespoons soy or sunflower oil
1/2 teaspoon mustard seeds
3/4 teaspoon cumin seeds

1/4 teaspoon sesame seeds
1 teaspoon minced garlic
1 teaspoon chopped lime pickle
1 teaspoon Homemade Curry
   Powder, page 6
1/4 cup (60g) canned mixed
   vegetables, liquid reserved
2 teaspoons chopped cilantro
Salt to taste

1. Bring stock or water to a boil, then add lentils, coconut, chile pepper and curry leaves, if using. Simmer 20 minutes. Spoon off froth that forms.
2. Heat oil in wok or large skillet. Stir-fry seeds 20 seconds. Add garlic, pickle and curry powder and stir-fry 1 minute. Add vegetables. When sizzling, add cilantro and vegetable liquid.
3. Add lentil mixture to wok. Simmer 2 to 3 minutes. Add salt.

Makes 2 servings.

Each serving contains:

Cal	Prot	Carb	Fib	Tot. Fat	Sat. Fat	Chol	Sodium
251	8g	23g	6g	16g	3g	0mg	321mg

CHICKPEA CURRY (CHOLE)

This recipe is based on a Kashmiri dish—*chole*, pronounced "cho-lay." Note the use of hummus as a thickener. Serve with a main-course curry, bread or rice and chutneys.

2 tablespoons clarified butter
1/2 teaspoon cumin seeds
1/4 teaspoon coriander seeds
2 cardamoms, halved
4 whole cloves, crushed
2 bay leaves
2 teaspoons chopped garlic
1 tablespoon chopped fresh ginger
1 can (14-oz. / 400g) chickpeas,
  drained, liquid reserved
2 teaspoons tomato purée
2 tablespoons butter

6 tablespoons dried onion flakes
1 teaspoon chopped mint
1/4 teaspoon vinegar
6-8 cherry tomatoes, halved
1 tablespoon chopped bell pepper
1-2 red chile peppers
1 tablespoon plain yogurt
2 tablespoons hummus (or more)
1 tablespoon chopped cilantro
1 teaspoon Garam Masala, page 5
Salt to taste

1. Heat clarified butter in wok or large skillet. Stir-fry seeds and spices 30 seconds; add garlic and ginger and stir-fry 1 to 2 minutes. Add 1 or 2 tablespoons chickpea liquid, then mix in tomato purée. Add butter and onion flakes and stir-fry 2 to 3 minutes.
2. Add another 1 to 2 teaspoons chickpea liquid, mint, vinegar, tomatoes and peppers. When mixture is sizzling, add chickpeas, yogurt and remaining chickpea liquid.
3. Add hummus to thicken the curry to desired consistency. Add cilantro, garam masala and salt. Remove and discard bay leaves.
4. Stir and simmer until hot.

Makes 2 servings.

Each serving contains:

Cal	Prot	Carb	Fib	Tot. Fat	Sat. Fat	Chol	Sodium
559	14g	67g	11g	29g	16g	64mg	921mg

QUICK TASTY DHAL

Lentil dishes, or *dhal,* are immensely popular in India. Serve with plain rice and chutneys for a nutritious, delicious, inexpensive and satisfying meal. I use split red lentils because they are the quickest to cook. Even so, this recipe has one of the longest cooking times in the book: 40 minutes.

*2/3 cup (160ml) canned
    consommé or water
1/3 cup (75g) split red lentils
3 tablespoons clarified butter
2 teaspoons chopped garlic
1 teaspoon chopped fresh ginger
3 tablespoons toasted onion flakes*

*1 tablespoon plain yogurt
2 tablespoons hummus
1 teaspoon dried fenugreek leaves
1 teaspoon Garam Masala, page 5
2 teaspoons ketchup
Salt to taste*

1. Bring consommé or water to a boil, add lentils and simmer 20 minutes.
2. Add remaining ingredients and simmer until desired texture. This takes about 20 minutes. Add more water if needed to keep dhal from sticking.

Makes 2 servings.

Each serving contains:

Cal	Prot	Carb	Fib	Tot. Fat	Sat. Fat	Chol	Sodium
352	13g	29g	6g	22g	12g	50mg	270mg

Chapter Nine

QUICK, EASY SAUCES

I've been considering pasta, one of the most popular cook-at-home foods. The reason for its success, I believe, is its simplicity. In one pan you boil the pasta, in another you make a sauce. They are both ready to eat in minutes and you simply combine one with the other for a marvelous meal.

Suppose we could do the same with curry. In one pan you cook the rice, in the other you create a tasty sauce. Forget about meat, chicken, fish, shrimp or vegetables. Just cook the sauce, in the time it takes to cook the rice, pour it over the rice (or pasta), mix it in and eat it.

Here are pour-and-mix sauce versions of 12 of the most popular restaurant curries.

CEYLONESE SAUCE

This restaurant-style interpretation of the tart, hot, coconut-creamy curries of Sri Lanka uses coconut milk, lime (fresh and pickled) and chili powder. Serve with plain or flavored rice.

3/4 cup (150g) basmati rice
2 tablespoons soy or sunflower oil
1 teaspoon mustard seeds
1 tablespoon Homemade Curry
*   Powder, page 6*
1/8 teaspoon asafetida (optional)
1 tablespoon chopped garlic
2 tablespoons water
6 tablespoons dried onion flakes,
*   crumbled*

2/3 cup (160ml) coconut milk
1 tablespoon grated coconut
10-12 curry leaves, fresh or dried
*   (optional)*
1 teaspoon finely chopped lime
*   pickle*
Salt to taste
Garnishes—lime juice, chili
*   powder, black pepper*

1. Cook rice according to one of the recipes in chapter 10.
2. Heat oil in wok or large skillet. Stir-fry mustard seeds 10 seconds. Add curry powder, asafetida, if using, and garlic. Stir-fry 1 minute. Add water and onion flakes. Mix in briskly, adding more water as needed to prevent burning.
3. Add coconut milk, coconut, curry leaves, if using, and lime pickle. Simmer a few minutes until sauce thickens. Add salt.
4. To serve, mix sauce into rice. Sprinkle with lime juice, chili powder and pepper.

Makes 2 servings.

Each serving contains:

Cal	Prot	Carb	Fib	Tot. Fat	Sat. Fat	Chol	Sodium
601	9g	74g	4g	33g	18g	0mg	257mg

DHANSAK SAUCE

This lentil-based curry is savory, hot and slightly sweet.

3/4 cup (150g) basmati rice
3 tablespoons clarified butter
1/2 teaspoon chili powder
1 teaspoon ground coriander
1/2 teaspoon ground cumin
1/4 teaspoon ground cinnamon
1/4 teaspoon fennel seeds
1/4 teaspoon cardamom seeds
1 teaspoon chopped garlic
2 teaspoons chopped fresh ginger
1 teaspoon raw or dark-brown
  sugar

4 tablespoons tomato juice
2 tablespoons dried onion flakes
1/2 cup (85g) canned ratatouille
  or mixed vegetables
1/3 cup (85g) canned chickpeas,
  mashed with their liquid
2-3 tablespoons hummus
2 tablespoons puréed spinach
1 teaspoon Garam Masala, page 5
Salt to taste
Garnishes—lemon juice,
  chopped cilantro

1. Cook rice according to one of the recipes in chapter 10.
2. Heat butter in wok or large skillet. Stir-fry spices, garlic and ginger 30 seconds. Add sugar and stir-fry 1 minute. Stir in tomato juice and onion.
3. Add ratatouille, chickpeas and hummus and mix in well, adding a little water if necessary. Stir and simmer 3 minutes.
4. Add spinach, garam masala and salt and simmer 2 to 3 minutes. Add water if sauce becomes too thick.
5. Mix sauce into rice and sprinkle with lemon juice and cilantro.

Makes 2 servings.

Each serving contains:

Cal	Prot	Carb	Fib	Tot. Fat	Sat. Fat	Chol	Sodium
568	11g	84g	5g	23g	13g	49mg	432mg

KASHMIRI SAUCE

Long ago, the owners of curry restaurants decided that Kashmiri curries contained fruit. They decided to use lychees—which come from China, not Kashmir! Authentic Kashmiri food uses lotus, not lychees. Nevertheless, here is a Kashmiri interpretation using canned lychees enhanced with aromatic spices.

3/4 cup (150g) basmati rice
3 tablespoons clarified butter
1 teaspoon white poppy seeds
2 teaspoons chopped garlic
1 teaspoon chopped fresh ginger
1 teaspoon white sugar
1/2 cup (125ml) tomato juice
4 tablespoons dried onion flakes

1 teaspoon pesto sauce
3/4 cup (185ml) milk
1 tablespoon ground almonds
4 canned lychees, chopped
1 tablespoon chopped cilantro
Salt to taste
Garnishes—Garam Masala, page 5,
   chopped mint

1. Cook rice according to one of the recipes in chapter 10.
2. Heat butter in wok or large skillet. Stir-fry poppy seeds 20 seconds. Add garlic, ginger and sugar and stir-fry 1 minute. Add half the tomato juice and the onion flakes and mix well. Add remaining tomato juice, pesto and milk.
3. Add almonds, lychees and cilantro and stir-fry until heated. Add salt to taste.
4. Mix sauce into rice and sprinkle with garam masala and mint.

Makes 2 servings.

Each serving contains:

Cal	Prot	Carb	Fib	Tot. Fat	Sat. Fat	Chol	Sodium
598	12g	84g	4g	26g	14g	57mg	424mg

KORMA SAUCE

The true *korma* is aromatic and mild because the meat is marinated in yogurt before being slow-cooked to a creamy result. This version uses evaporated milk, cream and coconut to achieve a rich, mild curry.

3/4 cup (150g) basmati rice
3 tablespoons clarified butter
3/4 teaspoon cumin seeds
1/2 teaspoon fennel seeds
1/4 teaspoon cardamom seeds
Cinnamon stick (1-inch / 2.5cm)
2 bay leaves
1-1/2 teaspoons minced garlic
1/2 teaspoon chopped fresh ginger
4 tablespoons water
6 tablespoons dried onion flakes

1/4 cup (60ml) cream
3 tablespoons evaporated milk
1/2 teaspoon saffron powder
1 tablespoon coconut-milk powder
2 teaspoons ground almonds
1 teaspoon Garam Masala, page 5
1 tablespoon chopped cilantro
Salt to taste
Garnish—1 tablespoon toasted
    sliced almonds

1. Cook rice according to one of the recipes in chapter 10.
2. Heat butter in wok or large skillet. Stir-fry seeds and spices 30 seconds. Add garlic and ginger and stir-fry 30 seconds. Add water and onion flakes, stirring constantly.
3. Mix in cream and evaporated milk and stir-fry 3 to 4 minutes, adding water if necessary.
4. Add remaining ingredients except sliced almonds and simmer 3 to 4 minutes. Remove and discard whole spices.
5. To serve, mix sauce into rice and garnish with toasted almonds.

Makes 2 servings.

Each serving contains:

Cal	Prot	Carb	Fib	Tot. Fat	Sat. Fat	Chol	Sodium
806	12g	77g	4g	53g	38g	76mg	189mg

MALAYSIAN SAUCE

Malaysian curries link Indian techniques with Chinese ingredients. This recipe produces a smooth, tangy curry with a sweet undertone.

3/4 cup (150g) basmati rice
2 tablespoons soy oil
1 teaspoon Bengali Five-Spice
    Mixture, page 7
1/2 teaspoon turmeric
2-3 cloves garlic, sliced
2-inch (5cm) piece ginger, sliced
1 tablespoon Homemade Curry
    Powder, page 6
6 tablespoons tomato juice
6 tablespoons toasted onion
    flakes, crumbled

1 tablespoon brinjal (eggplant)
    pickle, chopped
1 tablespoon peanut butter
6 tablespoons coconut milk
1 tablespoon creamed coconut,
    chopped, page 4
1-2 red chile peppers, chopped
12-20 cilantro leaves
4-6 canned pineapple chunks
Salt to taste
Garnishes—lemon juice,
    fresh cilantro

1. Cook rice according to one of the recipes in chapter 10.
2. Heat oil in wok or large skillet. Stir-fry five-spice mixture and turmeric 30 seconds. Add garlic and ginger and stir-fry 1 minute. Add curry powder and 2 tablespoons tomato juice and cook 30 seconds. Add onion flakes, brinjal pickle and remaining tomato juice and stir well 1 minute.
3. Add remaining ingredients except salt and garnishes and stir-fry 3 minutes.
4. Add salt and simmer 3 to 4 minutes. Add water if necessary to achieve a thin sauce.
5. Mix sauce into rice and sprinkle with lemon juice and cilantro.

Makes 2 servings.

Each serving contains:

Cal	Prot	Carb	Fib	Tot. Fat	Sat. Fat	Chol	Sodium
645	12g	90g	5g	31g	12g	0mg	408mg

MADRAS SAUCE

You won't find a *Madras* curry anywhere in Madras, but in Indian restaurants it has become synonymous with hot tasty curries.

3/4 cup (150g) basmati rice
3 tablespoons vegetable oil
1 tablespoon Homemade Curry
  Powder, page 6
1 teaspoon chili powder
2 teaspoons chopped garlic
1 teaspoon chopped fresh ginger
6 tablespoons toasted onion flakes
1 teaspoon dried fenugreek leaves
1 tablespoon tomato purée

1 tablespoon ketchup
4 canned tomatoes, chopped
1 tablespoon coconut-milk powder
1 tablespoon ground almonds
1 teaspoon white sugar
1 tablespoon chopped cilantro
Salt to taste
Garnishes—lemon juice, chili
  powder, twists of lemon peel

1. Cook rice according to one of the recipes in chapter 10.
2. Heat oil in wok or large skillet. Stir-fry curry powder and chili powder 1 minute, gradually adding 2 tablespoons water. Add garlic, ginger and more water if necessary to prevent sticking. Cook 1 minute.
3. Add onion flakes, fenugreek, tomato purée and ketchup and stir-fry briskly 1 minute. Add tomatoes, coconut-milk powder, almonds, sugar and just enough water to hold mixture together. Stir-fry 3 minutes. Add cilantro and salt to taste.
4. To serve, mix sauce into rice. Sprinkle with lemon juice and garnish with chili powder and twists of lemon peel.

Makes 2 servings.

Each serving contains:

Cal	Prot	Carb	Fib	Tot. Fat	Sat. Fat	Chol	Sodium
801	12g	89g	6g	49g	25g	0mg	571mg

MUGLAI SAUCE

The Moguls, who ruled in India during the 16th and 17th centuries, enjoyed opulent food. Serve this sauce with plain or flavored rice.

3/4 cup (150g) basmati rice
1/4 cup (60ml) milk
10-15 saffron strands
3 tablespoons clarified butter
2 tablespoons pine nuts
3/4 teaspoon cumin seeds
1-2 star anise
4-6 cardamom seeds
4-6 cloves
Cinnamon stick (1-inch / 2.5cm)
1 tablespoon chopped garlic

1 tablespoon Homemade Curry
   Powder, page 6
6 tablespoons cream
6 tablespoons toasted onion flakes
1 tablespoon ground almonds
4 mint leaves, chopped
10-12 cilantro leaves
1 teaspoon Garam Masala, page 5
1 teaspoon chopped mango chutney
Garnishes—20-30 toasted sliced
   almonds, cream

1. Cook rice according to one of the recipes in chapter 10.
2. Warm milk and saffron over low heat 30 seconds or in the microwave about 10 seconds. To infuse the color, mash strands with back of a spoon.
3. Heat butter in wok or large skillet. Stir-fry pine nuts 30 seconds. Add spices and stir-fry 30 seconds. Add garlic, curry powder and 2 tablespoons cream and stir-fry 1 minute. Add onion flakes and, when sizzling, saffron and milk. Stir-fry until mixture dries out.
4. Add remaining ingredients except garnishes. Stir-fry until hot, adding water if needed to hold sauce together. Remove and discard whole spices.
5. Mix sauce into rice and garnish with sliced almonds and cream.
Makes 2 servings.

Each serving contains:

Cal	Prot	Carb	Fib	Tot. Fat	Sat. Fat	Chol	Sodium
775	16g	81g	5g	47g	22g	91mg	56mg

PATIA SAUCE

Originally created centuries ago by the Parsees, patia combines heat and sweetness in a rich, dark-red sauce.

3/4 cup (150g) basmati rice
2 tablespoons clarified butter
1 teaspoon ground coriander
1/2 teaspoon ground cinnamon
1/4 teaspoon ground cloves
1 teaspoon Tandoori Curry
  Powder, page 7
1 teaspoon paprika
1/2-1 teaspoon chili powder
1 teaspoon minced garlic
2 teaspoons chopped fresh ginger
1 teaspoon raw or dark-brown
  sugar
2 tablespoons butter
6 tablespoons toasted onion flakes

2/3 cup (160ml) canned cream of
  tomato soup
1 teaspoon tomato purée
2 teaspoons ketchup
2 teaspoons mango chutney,
  chopped
1 teaspoon Dijon-style mustard
1 teaspoon horseradish sauce
1 teaspoon red pesto
1/2 teaspoon mint jelly
1 tablespoon chopped cilantro
1 teaspoon Garam Masala, page 5
Salt to taste
Garnishes—potato sticks, dried
  coconut

1. Cook rice according to one of the recipes in chapter 10.
2. Heat clarified butter in wok or large skillet. Stir-fry spices 1 minute, adding water if needed to keep them from sticking. Add garlic, ginger, sugar, butter and onion flakes. Stir-fry 2 to 3 minutes, gradually adding tomato soup.
3. Add remaining ingredients except garnishes. Stir-fry 2 to 3 minutes. Add a little water if necessary.
4. Mix sauce into rice. Garnish with potato sticks and coconut.

Makes 2 servings.

Each serving contains:

Cal	Prot	Carb	Fib	Tot. Fat	Sat. Fat	Chol	Sodium
687	10g	92g	4g	34g	20g	66mg	1096mg

PHAL SAUCE

Only in Indian restaurants will you find the hottest curry: *phal.*
Its potent red heat comes from extra-hot chili powder.

3/4 cup (150g) basmati rice
3 tablespoons vegetable oil
1 teaspoon cumin seeds
1 teaspoon paprika
2-3 teaspoons extra-hot chili
  powder
1 teaspoon Homemade Curry
  Powder, page 6
2 tablespoons water
2 teaspoons chopped garlic
1 tablespoon chopped chili pickle
6 tablespoons dried onion flakes,
  crumbled

6 tablespoons tomato juice
1 tablespoon ketchup
1-2 teaspoons minced red chile
  pepper
1 teaspoon prepared mustard
1/2 teaspoon dried mint
1 tablespoon chopped cilantro
Salt to taste
Garnish—1-2 green chile peppers,
  shredded

1. Cook rice according to one of the recipes in chapter 10.
2. Heat oil in wok or large skillet. Stir-fry cumin seeds, paprika,
   chili powder and curry powder. Add water, garlic and pickle.
   Stir-fry 1 minute.
3. Stir in onion flakes, then add tomato juice. Stir-fry 2 to 3 minutes,
   adding water if necessary. Add remaining ingredients except salt
   and garnish and bring to a simmer. Add salt to taste.
4. To serve, mix sauce into rice and garnish with chile peppers.

Makes 2 servings.

Each serving contains:

Cal	Prot	Carb	Fib	Tot. Fat	Sat. Fat	Chol	Sodium
524	8g	78g	3g	23g	3g	0mg	749mg

ROGHAN JOSH SAUCE

Roghan means "clarified butter" in Iranian and "red" in Kashmiri. This is a Mogul dish and as the Moguls spoke Persian and lived in Kashmir both meanings could apply. *Josh,* incidentally, means "sauce."

3/4 cup (150g) basmati rice
3 tablespoons clarified butter
3/4 teaspoon cumin seeds
2 cardamom pods, halved
2 bay leaves
3 cloves, crushed
1/2 teaspoon fennel seeds
1/2 teaspoon paprika
1/2 teaspoon ground coriander
2-3 cloves garlic, chopped
1-inch (2.5cm) piece fresh ginger, shredded
3/4 cup (185ml) milk

4 tablespoons dried onion flakes
1 tablespoon pickled beet, mashed
1/2 cup (125ml) canned cream of mushroom soup
1 tablespoon thinly sliced bell pepper
1 tablespoon thinly sliced green chile pepper
4 cherry tomatoes, quartered
1 tablespoon plain yogurt
1 tablespoon chopped cilantro
Salt to taste
Garnish—fresh cilantro

1. Cook rice according to one of the recipes in chapter 10.
2. Heat butter in wok or large skillet. Stir-fry spices 30 seconds. Add garlic and stir-fry 30 seconds. Add ginger and cook 30 seconds.
3. Add 3 tablespoons milk, onion flakes and beet. Gradually add remaining milk, stirring constantly. Add remaining ingredients except garnish. Stir and simmer 3 minutes. Discard bay leaves.
4. To serve, mix sauce into rice and garnish with cilantro.

Makes 2 servings.

Each serving contains:

Cal	Prot	Carb	Fib	Tot. Fat	Sat. Fat	Chol	Sodium
591	12g	79g	2g	27g	15g	58mg	725mg

THAI GREEN CURRY SAUCE

Look for this authentic dish at Thai restaurants. The sauce gets its color from green ingredients—peppers, cilantro and basil. The fragrance of Thai food comes largely from lemon grass and fresh basil.

3/4 cup (150g) basmati rice
2 tablespoons soy oil
2 teaspoons minced garlic
1 teaspoon minced fresh ginger
4-5 green onions (leaves and
   bulbs), sliced
2 pieces bottled or fresh lemon-
   grass stalk
1 tablespoon sliced green bell pepper
1-2 green chile peppers, chopped
1 teaspoon green pesto

1 tablespoon dried cilantro
1 tablespoon cooked shrimp,
   mashed (optional)
6 tablespoons coconut milk
10-12 fresh basil leaves, chopped
1 teaspoon light soy sauce
Salt to taste
2-3 limes
Garnish—1 large red chile pepper,
   shredded, or miniature chile
   peppers

1. Cook rice according to one of the recipes in chapter 10.
2. Heat oil in wok or large skillet. Stir-fry garlic and ginger 30 seconds. Add green onions and lemon grass; stir-fry 1 minute. Add peppers, pesto, cilantro and shrimp, if using, and stir-fry 1 minute.
3. Add coconut milk and simmer 2 to 3 minutes, stirring frequently, until slightly thickened.
4. Add basil, soy sauce and salt. Simmer and stir 2 minutes until leaves soften. Remove and discard lemon grass.
5. To serve, mix sauce into rice. Sprinkle with lime juice and garnish with chile peppers.

Makes 2 servings.

Each serving contains:

Cal	Prot	Carb	Fib	Tot. Fat	Sat. Fat	Chol	Sodium
529	9g	71g	3g	25g	11g	1mg	250mg

VINDALOO SAUCE

This dish originated in Portuguese Goa, where it combined vinegar and garlic with chile peppers. The restaurant interpretation latched onto the word *aloo,* meaning "potato," but dropped the vinegar.

3/4 cup (150g) basmati rice
3 tablespoons vegetable oil
2 teaspoons Homemade Curry Powder, page 6
1-2 teaspoons extra-hot chili powder
2 tablespoons water
2 teaspoons chopped garlic
1 teaspoon chopped chili pickle
6 tablespoons toasted onion flakes
2 canned tomatoes, chopped

1/2 cup (125ml) canned cream of tomato soup
1/2-1 teaspoon minced red chile pepper
1 tablespoon chopped cilantro
2-3 small cooked potatoes, halved (optional)
Salt to taste
Garnishes—cilantro, chopped green chile peppers

1. Cook rice according to one of the recipes in chapter 10.
2. Heat oil in wok or large skillet. Stir-fry curry powder and chili powder 1 minute, adding water gradually. Add garlic, pickle and more water, if needed to prevent sticking, and stir-fry 1 minute.
3. Add onion flakes and tomatoes and mix well. Gradually stir in tomato soup.
4. Add pepper, cilantro and potatoes, if using. Simmer 2 to 3 minutes, adding water if the sauce becomes too dry. Add salt to taste.
5. Mix sauce into rice and garnish with cilantro and chiles.

Makes 2 servings.

Each serving contains:

Cal	Prot	Carb	Fib	Tot. Fat	Sat. Fat	Chol	Sodium
554	9g	83g	3g	23g	4g	0mg	828mg

Chapter Ten

RICE

Rice does not take a lot of time to cook—less than 10 minutes, including rinsing. But to get fluffy grains, you will have to allow at least 30 minutes for it to dry out after cooking. If you cook rice the day before and keep it in the refrigerator you can reheat it quickly by stir-frying. It can also be frozen successfully—just stir-fry the thawed rice and it will be almost as good as new. On the other hand, I sometimes eat my rice immediately after straining it and it is quite acceptable.

Curry and rice go together like sun and sky, and we can scarcely imagine one without the other. But there are parts of India where the climate is wrong for growing rice and only bread is eaten with curries. Pita bread can be substituted for the Indian bread, *naan,* and warmed in a toaster.

PLAIN BOILED RICE

Using basmati rice, follow this recipe accurately and you will have fragrant, fluffy dry rice.

3/4 cup (150g) basmati rice   *3-1/2 cups (875ml) water*

1. Rinse rice with cold water until most of the starch is washed out and the water runs clear.
2. Bring 3-1/2 cups water to a boil in a large saucepan. It is not necessary to salt it.
3. To minimize temperature reduction, rinse rice a final time with hot water.
4. Add rice to pan and start timing. Cover pan until water returns to a boil, then remove the lid and stir frequently.
5. After about 6 minutes, taste a few grains. As soon as the center is no longer brittle, but still has a good *al dente* bite to it, strain off the water. The rice will be slightly undercooked. It takes 8 to 10 minutes from the time you put the rice in the pan.
6. Shake off excess water, then place the strainer on a dry towel to remove the last of the water.
7. After a minute or so, place the rice in a warmed serving dish. You can serve it now or, preferably, put it in a warm oven for at least 30 minutes, but not longer than 90 minutes. As the rice dries, the grains separate and become fluffy.
8. Before serving, fluff rice with a fork.

Makes 2 servings.

Each serving contains:

Cal	Prot	Carb	Fib	Tot. Fat	Sat. Fat	Chol	Sodium
268	6g	60g	0g	1g	0g	0mg	0mg

FRIED PULLAO RICE

Pullao is a combination of rice and meat or vegetables cooked together. Any of the variations can be made into a meal by adding a curry sauce and serving with a side dish of chutney.

2 teaspoons clarified butter	*1 bay leaf*
1/2 teaspoon fennel seeds	*1-2 cloves*
1/4 teaspoon cardamom seeds	*3/4 cup (150g) basmati rice,*
1/4 teaspoon cumin seeds	*cooked, page 102*
1 star anise	*1/2 teaspoon saffron powder*
Cinnamon stick (1-inch / 2.5cm)	*Garnish—dried coconut*

1. Heat butter in wok or large skillet and stir-fry spices, except saffron, 30 seconds.
2. Lower heat, add cooked rice and saffron powder and stir-fry briskly until heated. Remove and discard bay leaf and other large spices. Garnish with coconut and serve at once.

Makes 2 servings.

Variations

Pea Pullao Rice—Add 3 tablespoons cooked peas.

Mushroom Pullao Rice—Add 4 to 6 chopped mushrooms.

Garlic Pullao Rice—Add 1 tablespoon chopped garlic to spice mixture.

Pickle Pullao Rice—Add 1 to 2 tablespoons chopped Indian pickle (lime, mango, brinjal or mixed).

Cachumber Rice—Add 1 recipe Cachumber Salad Chutney, page 111.

Rice and Chickpeas (Kitchri)—Add 1/4 cup (60g) cooked chickpeas.

Each serving (basic recipe) contains:

Cal	Prot	Carb	Fib	Tot. Fat	Sat. Fat	Chol	Sodium
338	6g	61g	1g	8g	6g	11mg	2mg

CHICKEN TIKKA PULLAO

This variation of Fried Pullao Rice could become your favorite. You will need cooked Chicken Tikka, page 30. It is good accompanied by Quick Tasty Dhal, page 85, and chutneys.

1 tablespoon clarified butter
1/2 teaspoon cumin seeds
2 teaspoons Tandoori Curry Powder, page 7
2 green onions (leaves and bulbs), chopped
1/2 tablespoon chopped bell pepper
1 green chile pepper, chopped (optional)
2 tablespoons yogurt

1 teaspoon tomato purée
1-1/4 cups (280g) Chicken Tikka, page 30, cut small
1-1/2 cups (300g) Fried Pullao Rice, page 103
1 tablespoon chopped cilantro
1 teaspoon Garam Masala, page 5
Salt to taste
Garnishes—snipped chives, sliced almonds

1. Heat butter in wok or large skillet. Fry cumin seeds and curry powder 10 seconds.
2. Add green onions and peppers and stir-fry 3 minutes. Add yogurt and tomato purée and stir-fry 1 minute.
3. Add chicken tikka and stir-fry 3 minutes.
4. Add pullao rice and stir-fry carefully until heated.
5. Add cilantro and garam masala and stir-fry 2 to 3 minutes, then add salt to taste. Garnish with chives and almonds and serve.

Makes 2 servings.

Each serving contains:

Cal	Prot	Carb	Fib	Tot. Fat	Sat. Fat	Chol	Sodium
533	20g	68g	3g	21g	9g	59mg	576mg

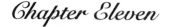

Chapter Eleven

CHUTNEYS

Serious curryholics collect bottled Indian pickles. The usual ones are lime, brinjal (eggplant) and mango pickles. There is also a mixed version of these, as well as a chili pickle for those who like it hot. On the mild side, there is mango chutney, more familiar to most of us. These pickles vary quite markedly from manufacturer to manufacturer. It is a good idea to have some of these ready-made items in your cupboard. I use them for cooking as well as for enjoying in their own right.

But India has much more up her sleeve to accompany curries: freshly made chutneys. That's what the following recipes are all about. They are quick to make, and go so well with the recipes in this book that you could have more than one with each meal.

DANA PODINE PURÉE

A tasty, herby chutney.

2-3 green onions (leaves and
  bulbs), finely chopped
1 teaspoon dried cilantro

1/2 teaspoon chopped mint
1/4 teaspoon vinegar

Combine all ingredients. Add enough water to hold together.
Makes 2 servings.

Each serving contains:

Cal	Prot	Carb	Fib	Tot. Fat	Sat. Fat	Chol	Sodium
5	0g	1g	0g	0g	0g	0mg	3mg

COCONUT CHUTNEY

Coconut is soothing; red pepper adds a bite.

1/2 teaspoon nigella (black seeds)
4 tablespoons dried coconut
1 tablespoon coconut-milk powder

4 tablespoons milk
1 teaspoon crushed red pepper
1 teaspoon ketchup

Mix nigella, dried coconut, coconut-milk powder and milk. Let
soak for 10 minutes, then stir in remaining ingredients.
Makes 2 servings.

Each serving contains:

Cal	Prot	Carb	Fib	Tot. Fat	Sat. Fat	Chol	Sodium
305	4g	8g	3g	31g	27g	2mg	64mg

Opposite: Chicken Tikka Masala Curry (page 32) on Fried Pullao Rice (page 103)
served with Aloo Ghobi Sag (page 81) and an Indian bread

GREEN CHILE CHUTNEY

This is easy to make and keeps indefinitely. Although its bright-green color will fade over time, the flavor remains unchanged.

Reminder: Watch where you put your hands after chopping the chiles. They can be killers if you touch your eyes after handling them. Some people wear kitchen gloves when chopping chiles, as they can make your fingertips burn too.

2 green chile peppers, seeded and chopped	1/2 cup (125ml) vinegar (any type)

1. Use blender to purée chile peppers and vinegar.
2. Store in an airtight jar.

Makes 2 servings.

Variation

Red Chile Chutney—Use red chiles instead of green. The same safety comments apply.

Each serving contains:

Cal	Prot	Carb	Fib	Tot. Fat	Sat. Fat	Chol	Sodium
26	1g	8g	1g	0g	0g	0mg	4mg

Opposite: Stir-Fried Shashlik (page 49) served with Plain Boiled Rice (page 102) and Red Chile Chutney (above)

BALTI RED RAITA

Bright-red yogurt chutney is a common accompaniment to baltis.

6 tablespoons plain yogurt
1 teaspoon Tandoori Curry
   Powder, page 7
1/2 teaspoon tomato purée

1 teaspoon ketchup
1/4 teaspoon dried mint
1/2 teaspoon crushed red pepper
   (optional)

1. Combine all ingredients.
2. Chill if you have time, or serve at once.

Makes 2 servings.

Each serving contains:

Cal	Prot	Carb	Fib	Tot. Fat	Sat. Fat	Chol	Sodium
36	2g	4g	0g	2g	1g	6mg	132mg

TANDOORI GREEN RAITA

Green yogurt chutney contrasts well with red tandooris and tikkas.

6 tablespoons plain yogurt
2 teaspoons minced green
   bell pepper
1/2 teaspoon minced green
   chile pepper

1/2 teaspoon dried cilantro
1/2 teaspoon chopped mint
1/8 teaspoon vinegar
6-8 drops green food coloring
   (optional)

1. Combine all ingredients in a nonmetallic bowl.
2. Chill if you have time, or serve at once.

Makes 2 servings.

Each serving contains:

Cal	Prot	Carb	Fib	Tot. Fat	Sat. Fat	Chol	Sodium
29	2g	2g	0g	2g	1g	6mg	21mg

CURRY YELLOW RAITA

Garnish with red peppers for a color contrast.

1 tablespoon sesame oil
1/2 teaspoon mustard seeds
1/2 teaspoon turmeric
6 tablespoons plain yogurt

1 tablespoon minced yellow
* bell pepper*
1/2 teaspoon yellow food coloring

1. Heat oil in a skillet. Sauté mustard seeds and turmeric
   10 seconds. Remove from heat and put into a bowl.
2. Add remaining ingredients, stir well and allow to cool.
3. Chill if you have time, or serve at once.

Makes 2 servings.

Each serving contains:

Cal	Prot	Carb	Fib	Tot. Fat	Sat. Fat	Chol	Sodium
89	2g	2g	0g	8g	2g	6mg	21mg

WHITE COCONUT RAITA

This mixture of yogurt and coconut is a cool accompaniment to curry.

5 tablespoons plain yogurt
1 tablespoon whipping cream
1 tablespoon dried coconut

2 tablespoons coconut-milk
* powder*
1 teaspoon sesame seeds

1. Combine all ingredients.
2. Chill if you have time, or serve at once.

Makes 2 servings.

Each serving contains:

Cal	Prot	Carb	Fib	Tot. Fat	Sat. Fat	Chol	Sodium
510	6g	9g	3g	54g	47g	15mg	51mg

GARAM BROWN RAITA

Garam masala gives a pretty beige color and a gorgeous aromatic flavor.

6 tablespoons plain yogurt   *1 tablespoon Garam Masala, page 5*

1. Combine yogurt and garam masala.
2. Chill if you have time, or serve at once.

Makes 2 servings.

Each serving contains:

Cal	Prot	Carb	Fib	Tot. Fat	Sat. Fat	Chol	Sodium
48	2g	6g	2g	2g	1g	6mg	26mg

ONION BALTI CHUTNEY

This chutney uses green food coloring as well as green ingredients.

2-3 green onions (leaves only), minced
1/2 teaspoon fresh mint
1/8 teaspoon vinegar

1 tablespoon minced green bell pepper
2-3 drops green food coloring

1. Combine all ingredients in a nonmetallic bowl.
2. Chill if you have time, or serve at once.

Makes 2 servings.

Each serving contains:

Cal	Prot	Carb	Fib	Tot. Fat	Sat. Fat	Chol	Sodium
6	0g	1g	0g	0g	0g	0mg	3mg

CACHUMBER SALAD CHUTNEY

This chutney is one of the best accompaniments to curry because its fresh, raw onion cuts through the rich sauces.

1/2 small onion, thinly sliced
1 teaspoon finely chopped red bell
  pepper
1/2 teaspoon finely chopped green
  chile pepper

1/2 teaspoon chopped mint
1/8 teaspoon vinegar
1 tablespoon lemon juice
1/2 teaspoon paprika

Combine all ingredients and serve.

Makes 2 servings.

Each serving contains:

Cal	Prot	Carb	Fib	Tot. Fat	Sat. Fat	Chol	Sodium
9	0g	2g	0g	0g	0g	0mg	1mg

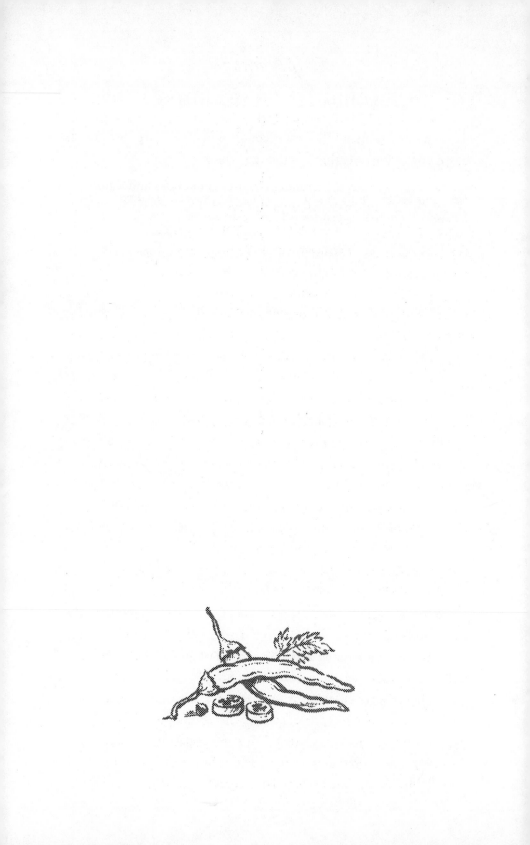

Appendix

THE CURRY CLUB

Pat Chapman, the founder of The Curry Club, is a world traveler and the author of 12 books, including 10 curry cookbooks and a guide to the 1000 best Indian restaurants in Britain. He always had a deep-rooted interest in spicy food, curry in particular, and over the years built up a huge pool of information. In order to share this with others with similar interests, he conceived the idea of The Curry Club.

Since it was founded in January 1982, The Curry Club has built up a membership of several thousand—including a marchioness, some lords and ladies, knights a-plenty, a captain of industry or two, generals, admirals and air marshals (not to mention a sprinkling of ex-colonels). There are celebrity names—actresses, politicians, rock stars and sportsmen—and an airline (Air India), a former Royal Navy warship (HMS Hermes) and a hotel chain (the Taj group).

Members come from every continent and include a typical cross-section of people, ranging in age from teenage to dotage, and in occupation from trash collectors to stock brokers, high-court judges to taxi drivers. There are students and retirees, millionaires and unemployed people—thousands of people who have just one thing in common—a love of curry and spicy foods.

Membership is open to anyone, but a special listing is made of those with relevant names. A recent count showed 15 members whose name is Curry or Currie, 20 called Rice and several with the name Spice or Spicer, Cook, Fry, Frier or Fryer and one Boiling. There is a Puri, a Paratha and a Nan, one Dal and a Lentil, an Oiler, a Gee (but no Ghee) and a Butter.

Members receive a colorful quarterly magazine with regular features on curry and the curry lands. It includes news items, recipes, reports on restaurants, picture features, and contributions from members and professionals alike. The information is largely concerned with curry, but by popular demand it now includes regular input on other exotic and spicy cuisines, such as those of the Middle East and China.

Obtaining some of the ingredients required for curry cooking may require a bit of looking, but The Curry Club makes it easy, with a comprehensive range of Curry Club products, including spice mixes, chutneys, pickles, pappadums, sauces and curry pastes. These can be ordered through the Club's well-established and efficient mail-order service. Hundreds of items are stocked, including spices, pickles, pastes, dry foods, canned foods, gift items, publications and specialty kitchen and tableware.

On the social side, the Club holds residential weekend cooking classes and gourmet nights at selected restaurants. At the top of the list are the Curry Club gourmet trips, on which a small group of curry enthusiasts visits the incredible sights of India or another "spicy" country, in between sampling the delicious foods of each region.

For more information about The Curry Club, write to:

THE CURRY CLUB
P.O. BOX 7
HASLEMERE, SURREY GU27 1EP
ENGLAND

For North Americans, approximate membership costs in The Curry Club are:

	Surface Mail	Air Mail
New Member	$33 U.S. (£21)	$69 U.S. (£44)
Renewal	$31 U.S. (£20)	$60 U.S. (£38)

GLOSSARY

A

Achar—East Indian word meaning "pickle."

Aloo—East Indian word meaning "potato."

Am—East Indian word meaning "mango."

Amchoor (mango powder)—powder made from sun-dried, unripe mangoes and used to give acidity to curry dishes. If unavailable, 1 teaspoon mango powder can be replaced with 2 tablespoons lemon juice.

Asafetida—pungent spice used sparingly in Asian cooking to add flavor and to aid in digestion. If unavailable, it can be omitted.

B

Balti—stir-fry; originally marinated meat cubes, charcoal-grilled, then simmered in sauce.

Basil—member of the mint family, with a pungent flavor. It is widely used in Thai cooking.

Basmati rice—long-grained, fine-textured rice with a nutlike flavor and aroma; grown in the foothills of the Himalayas and aged to reduce its moisture content.

Bay leaves—dried leaves of an evergreen, the bay laurel tree; usually not eaten, but used to flavor stews and other dishes. Often ground for use in Indian spice mixtures.

Bhaji—mild, somewhat dry, vegetable curry.

Bhuna—process of cooking a spice paste in oil.

Brinjal—East Indian word meaning "eggplant."

C

Cachumber—salad, dressed to be a cool accompaniment to curries; uses ginger and raw onion plus other vegetables and seasonings.

Cardamom—aromatic spice related to ginger. Seeds may be removed from pods before using, or pod and seeds ground up together. A common ingredient in curry powders.

Celery seeds—seeds of the wild celery plant. A small amount gives a slight celery taste, but it can be bitter.

Chile peppers—red or green capsicum peppers used to add heat to curries. Generally, small peppers are hotter than larger ones. Red chiles may be purchased fresh or dried. Red chile powder should be purchased ready-made; grinding your own releases a fine powder that can be very irritating to eyes, nose and throat.

Chili powder—may refer to pure ground chiles or to a mixture of chiles and other ingredients such as cumin and oregano. In Indian cooking, use ground chiles or cayenne.

Chole—chickpea curry.

Chutney—spicy condiment used as an accompaniment to curried dishes. Usually a combination of fruit, vinegar, sugar and spices.

Cilantro—fresh coriander, an herb used widely in Indian cooking. It may also be purchased dried.

Cinnamon—aromatic spice, the bark of an evergreen tree. It is used whole, as cinnamon stick, or ground.

Clarified butter—*see* Ghee.

Cloves—dried, unopened flower buds of an evergreen tree. Used whole in rice dishes and ground in curry spice mixtures.

Coconut—important ingredient in the curries of tropical regions. It can be purchased in many forms, the two used in this book being dried and creamed. Creamed coconut is a combination of freshly grated coconut meat and coconut oil and may be difficult to find. For a substitute, *see page 4*.

Coconut milk—white liquid squeezed from shredded coconut, *not* the liquid inside a fresh coconut. *See* page 4 for recipe.

Coriander—relative of parsley, the fresh leaves of this plant are known as *cilantro*. Coriander seeds, whole and ground, are important in garam masala and in flavoring curries.

Cumin—amber-colored, aromatic, dried fruit of a plant of the parsley family, used whole and ground in curry dishes.

Curry leaves—small, shiny leaves, similar in appearance to bay leaves, but giving off a strong curry fragrance when bruised. Difficult to find in U.S. and Canada, but easily grown in a pot.

Curry powder—mixture of spices used in Indian cooking. There is no standard recipe for curry powder—an Indian cook will grind different combinations daily, depending on the dishes to be cooked.

D

Dasai—pancake with stuffing.

Dhal—East Indian name for lentils, mung beans and other pulses.

Dhansak—dish involving purée of lentils, eggplant, tomato and spinach.

Dopiaza—dish utilizing two ("do") forms of onion ("piaza"): some fried at beginning of preparation, some added raw later on.

F

Fennel seeds—small green seeds, aromatic with aniseed taste.

Fenugreek—pungent herb, used as seeds and as fresh or dried leaves. An important ingredient in Indian cooking, it is considered essential to curries, especially those containing seafood.

G

Garam masala—East Indian term meaning "hot mixture of spices." A blend of ground spices that varies from cook to cook and from dish to dish. Its basic ingredients are black pepper, coriander, cumin, cloves and cinnamon.

Garlic—member of the lily family (as are onions and leeks), garlic is best purchased fresh, in the form of a bulb consisting of several cloves. Generally, the largest cloves are the sweetest. May also be purchased in bottles, minced or as a powder.

Ghee—East Indian form of clarified butter, which is butter from which the milk solids have been removed. *See* page 4 for recipe.

Ghobi—East Indian word meaning "cauliflower."

Ginger—rhizome which can be used fresh, dried or powdered. When fresh it looks like a thick, knobby root. To use, scrape off the light-brown skin and cut up as directed.

H

Hasina kebab—chicken, lamb or beef pieces marinated in spices then skewered and barbecued with onions, peppers and tomatoes.

Hoisin sauce—dark-brown, thick, sweet condiment made from soybeans.

Hummus—creamy sauce made of ground chickpeas and seasonings.

J

Jalfrezi—sautéed or stir-fried meat or chicken dish, often with onions, garlic, ginger and capsicum peppers. Originally "dry-fried" leftover cooked meat.

Jeera—East Indian name for cumin.

Josh—East Indian word meaning "sauce."

K

Karahi—Indian equivalent of a wok, a two-handled pan used for stir-frying, simmering, frying and deep-frying. Also known as a *balti pan.*

Keema—ground-meat curry.

Kitchri—dish made from chickpeas or lentils and rice.

Kofta—ground meat or vegetable balls in batter, deep-fried then cooked in a curry sauce.

Korma—very rich curry consisting of meat or vegetables cooked in cream, yogurt, and nuts with saffron and other aromatic spices.

L

Lemon grass—long thick, fragrant-leafed plant with lemony taste. Can be purchased fresh, dried or ground; 1 teaspoon ground is equivalent to 1 fresh stalk.

M

Madras—name given to hot curries.

Mango powder—*see* Amchoor.

Masala—East Indian name for curry powder.

Mint—herb used both fresh and dried. There are many varieties of mint, but spearmint is the one most commonly used in cooking.

Muglai Sauce—cooking in the style of the Mogul emperors.

Murgh—East Indian word meaning "chicken."

Mustard seeds—small seeds of the mustard plant, they become somewhat sweet when fried. When ground, they are sold as dry mustard.

N

Naan—flat bread, teardrop-shaped, 8-10 inches (20-25cm) long; baked in a tandoor oven.

Nigella or black seeds—seeds with slight onion flavor. May be difficult to find in U.S. and Canada.

O

Onion flakes—dried shredded onions; may also be purchased toasted.

P

Paneer—cheese made from cow or buffalo milk; can be fried and curried. Resembles cottage cheese.

Pappadum—thin Indian bread made from lentil flour, sold plain or seasoned with garlic, chiles or black pepper.

Paprika—red powder made from chile peppers. May be "sweet" or "hot," depending on the variety of pepper used.

Patia—Parsee curry with a thick brown sweet-sour sauce.

Pepper—whole or ground berries of the *Piper nigrum* plant. Fresh green peppercorns may be purchased freeze-dried or bottled in water or vinegar. Black peppercorns are underripe berries that have been dried; white peppercorns are mature berries from which outer skin has been removed.

117

Pesto—uncooked paste made from fresh basil, cheese, garlic, pine nuts and oilve oil. Best purchased fresh or frozen.

Phal—curry dish created by Indian restauranteurs; uses extra-hot chili powder.

Poppy seeds, white—seeds used in curries as a thickener. White poppy seeds have a nutlike flavor similar to that of the more-common black seeds, but are preferred in Indian cooking.

Prawn balichow—spicy Indian relish made from ground prawns (shrimp), onions, green chiles and seasonings. It may be difficult to find in the U.S. and Canada. Mango chutney may be substituted for it.

Pullao rice—rice and meat or vegetables cooked together with spices.

R

Raita—cooked chutney of vegetables or fruit and yogurt; used to complement a hot main dish.

Ratatouille—vegetable stew consisting of equal amounts of eggplant, zucchini, tomatoes and onions.

Roghan josh sauce—lamb marinated in yogurt, then cooked with ghee, spices and tomato. Creamy, spicy, not too hot.

S

Saffron—dried stamens of a variety of crocus, available as whole strands or powdered; adds flavor and a yellow tint to dishes.

Sag—East Indian word meaning "spinach."

Sag gosht—East Indian term meaning "spinach and meat."

Sambar—Indian combination of vegetables, lentils and chile peppers.

Sesame seeds—seeds of an Indonesian herb, widely used in Indian cooking.

Shashlik—cubes of marinated meat threaded onto skewers with chunks of onion and pepper, then broiled.

Sheek kebab (shish kebab)—spiced ground meat on skewers, traditionally cooked in a clay oven.

Star anise—star-shaped pod containing one seed in each of its eight arms. Has a slight licorice flavor similar to that of regular anise, but comes from a plant in the magnolia family.

T

Tandoori—meat marinated and skewered, baked at high temperature in brick-and-clay oven. Usually served in reddened yogurt sauce.

Tikka—skewered meat, marinated then barbecued.

Turmeric—powdered root of a plant related to ginger, common in Indian cooking. Has a slightly musty flavor and a thickening effect in liquids, but used primarily for its bright yellow color.

V

Vindaloo—fiery hot dish from Goa. Originally pork marinated in vinegar, garlic and chile peppers. Now any very hot dish, usually including potatoes (*aloo*) as an ingredient.

INDEX